Performing
Inside Out

D1596710

Performing
Inside Out

William Pennell Rock

A Stuart Abelson Book

Between Two Worlds Press
Chicago, Illinois

Distributed by Brick House Publishing Company
Acton, Massachusetts

Library of Congress Cataloging-in-Publication Data

Rock, William Pennell
    Performing Inside Out / William Pennell Rock.
        p.   cm.
    "A Stuart Abelson Book"
    ISBN 0-931790-10-7
    1. Performing arts—Religious aspects.   I. Title.
PN1647. R63   1990
291.3'7—dc20   90-39389
                                    CIP

Contents

Prologue

In the early seventies when I and several others were going through the illuminating ordeals of Oscar Ichazo's Arica training, our group was given an assignment called the "Three-Day Prayer." Like many other exercises and meditations in this mystical school, it was a task that seemed impossible before we did it and wondrous afterwards. Each of us had to practice the assignment in isolation on three successive days. The instruction was to lie face down for twelve hours, focusing awareness on the blood and its circulation through the body. On one of these days, our contemplation was to be enhanced with yage, a South American plant with psychedelic properties.

I did enter the blood. I disappeared into the body. For hours I was the cells being born out of the pelvic marrow, the heart pumping, the lungs circulating, the arteries pulsating, the veins, the capillaries, the infinite minute exchanges at the cellular level by which this body is vitalized, nourished and cleansed. I often found myself weeping at the beauty of it, at the overwhelming sadness that I had been so blind and unaware of the ongoing miracle sustained by this moment to moment life within me, the awesome truth that nature, earth and God are coursing through my being, loving me, caring for me, sustaining me. I begged the Source that I be forgiven for this forgetting. I committed myself irrevocably to the source of my being and the miraculous holiness of my body as Mother Earth.

The realization came that the experience of the body is a supreme religious image, the contemplation of which (largely unheard of in the Christian tradition) is an awesome medium of religious truth. I felt chagrin at my merely intellectual understanding of other traditions and their ways. And I was grateful for the deepest mystical truth directly expressed in the contemplation of the body as it simply, actually is.

What is the blood?

It is the plasma with its cells created out of the marrow of the femur and the pelvis. It flows through our lungs, our heart and our veins cleansing our cells, fighting for them, nourishing them, bringing them life moment to moment.

The poets tell us that blood is our passion, our vitality, our life essence.

1

The poets tell us that blood is our passion, our vitality, our life essence. The blood is a matter of life and death.

When Jesus gave of his blood to drink, it was his body essence as the living spirit of the Christ. It was the medium of transport into the optimal pattern of the divine human prototype. It was the way to commune with Christ, to return to the God-state that is our source, but from which we have fallen.

And this blood I came to know as the essence of vitality, of cleansing, of nourishing life in each individual cell. In my wonder, I saw that, despite our secularized reality, the gods have not fled. They are coursing through my veins in every moment of nature. It is just that I am inured to their presence... blinded by all I know as a civilized human being.

Preface

Theater is in my blood.

My mother was a real opera singer. My father was always on the Opera Board.

First, for me, there was dress-up. Then little dances and shows I used to do with my sister. We once performed a dance routine on television—I was the litterbug and she the trashcan imploring me to behave—that received rave reviews.

Moving into the big time, I would gather the neighborhood kids together to make little plays. Once we even made a movie.

There was a satisfaction and vitality to all of this that felt like home: It was in and of me, in and of our neighborhood. It was a threshold where our lives entered into some magical, mythological world—a doorway into some special and satisfying kind of truth.

It soon became obvious that I was a "natural." If you told me to get on the stage and do something—anything—I would throw myself into the part, and the audience believed it.

From school plays and such, I moved on to Johns Hopkins Children's Theater in Baltimore. Once, when playing Tom Sawyer, my part was so long that I ended up having to drift over to the wings from time to time in order to be prompted.

In other productions, there were no memorized lines. We would dramatize a fairy tale or some other story. The production would be all decked out with sets and costumes, but it would be improvised. The sense of vitality and danger I felt in this spontaneous way of doing things was noticeably different from what I felt when it was tight and memorized. Even then, craft, for me, was secondary to expression.

As a child actor, I progressed into adult community theater and then rapidly up the scale into professional theater, where I toured with the likes of Billie Burke and Basil Rathbone.

By the time I got to Yale University in 1959 and had been in dozens of plays, it seemed a foregone conclusion that I would have a life in theater.

But something else was going on. I began resenting the time taken from my studies for rehearsals. The fact is—and it took me a long time to realize this—I had become bored with theater. It seemed to me a great big fabrication, something carefully and safely crafted and then set up in front of people in order to distract them. It was not real.

The proscenium was exciting in a way, but it was also false. I felt that it was a separation between myself and the audience. I could not even see them. They would disappear behind the bright lights. The proscenium became a barrier for me, an alienation.

And this business of building a character: I called it "mask-making"— creating an illusory character to fill someone else's conception. Make this gesture a little more realistic. Change that movement a little. It was a kind of technology of controlled appearance. Again, as with the proscenium, it seemed as though I was engaged in fabricating a mere illusion.

Long gone was the quickening I felt as a child when we made up our plays *right there* and entered into a kind of spiritual wonder with those who happened to be present. Gone was the invigorating danger we had experienced, not knowing what would happen next. It had all become pre-packaged, prepared—denatured.

Theater was still in my blood. But the theater itself I now found bloodless.

Not so my studies. At least not the realms into which I was drawn. They were beckoning me further and further on a quest for truth. I was making a beeline toward the Mysteries. Of course, I had to go the academic routes, which often seemed arduous detours. But I was definitely hooked and hankering for the lifeblood, the greatest—the true quality of the Self.

My intuition told me what to do, though it was often at odds with my academic advisors. I was looking for the most ancient, that which remains in the depths of the present. I was looking for the source, the Origins.

Two words especially fascinated me: "primal," the archaic first beginnings, and "primordial," the first beginnings here-now in the present. Long before I reached any real understanding of where my passionate search was taking me, I had given up theater, because theater as it was known had nothing to do with the primal or the primordial.

My attraction to the primordial Self drew me with enthusiasm into psychological studies at Yale, but I soon felt weighed down by scientific method and a lot of intellectual apparatus. My intuition would speed toward conclusions and insights far more swiftly than the scientific method could follow. But I persevered, finding ways to allow more inquiry into the theories of the psyche.

Early in these academic studies I came upon Freud. For months I was psychoanalyzing everyone, including myself. But I soon sensed I was getting no further than Vienna during the oppression of Victoria. The problem was that Freudian psychology deals not with the primordial Self, but with the pathology of repression. It is remarkable to that extent, but not enough for me. It is not the true Origins.

One day, while searching the stacks of the Yale library, I came upon some dusty volumes of the works of Carl Jung. At that time, in the early sixties, Jung was definitely *non grata* in the context of Yale's academic values. As I read these volumes, however, my real sense of Self and mystery was stimulated as it had never been before. I knew in some way that, for the first time, Yale values notwithstanding, I was on the right track.

Of particular interest was myth. Through the works of Jung and the Jungian anthropologist Joseph Campbell it became clear that myths and dreams from all over the world are not just randomly variable, but actually contain patterns and similarities of form. Here was something primordial to contemplate. How could cultures and individuals, separated indubitably by time and space, still come up with the same basic forms? Why were they the same? And what was the meaning?

Joseph Campbell's book, *The Hero with a Thousand Faces,* set me on a fortuitous track. In this seminal work, he showed that the basic themes of myths, dreams and legends, from time immemorial to last night, record the basic way or path of every human psyche. Every human being is a Hero, and the Self is his quest. This became for me the basis of a real archeology of the soul, a true science of the Origins. I wrote an abstruse honors thesis about the Hero monomyth, the Self, and the meeting of conscious and unconscious. I called it *The Hero's Journey: A Study in Depth Synthesis.*

I had been brought up in a strong Methodist tradition. I loved religion, but I found nothing very illuminating in the Christianity I was being fed. It was all rather like my disillusionment with the theater. Church was something make-believe that everyone did, but it had little or nothing to do with the blood coursing through *my* veins.

When I realized, however, that religion is actually a sort of highly evolved mythology, I wanted to generalize the understanding achieved through my work on myth and look at religion from a similar point of view.

When I was raised as a Methodist, I had been taught there is no question that Christianity is the only religion—with only slight latitude given for other denominations. But I could no longer accept that, just because I had been brought up in a Christian tradition, Christianity was the only true religion! That seemed to be a very low-grade fallacy. What about little Ibrahim from Baghdad or little Jyoti from Jabalpur? No, I decided: If there is a fundamental pattern to all myths, there must be one to all religions. Increased knowledge of this prototype religion would, by definition, bring me closer to that primordial one Self we all are. Thus, when I won a fellowship to study comparative religions at Harvard in 1963, I went for it.

A year of study at Harvard convinced me that my intuitive sense was correct. There is only one true Mystery. Each of the great religions is a language expressing a certain point of view on that truth. Each has its own way of expressing Being and its laws. Just as each person has a native language through which he can best express himself and understand others, so each has a native religion. In this sense, each religion is the best.

At the same time, some things are better said in some religious languages and other things in other languages. I found that in each great religion there is something truly outstanding and beyond the capacity of other religions to express. For instance, Zen deals so beautifully with the true non-articulability or non-thingness of what we call "God." And Jesus' teaching is the most sophisticated statement of the truth and dynamic of forgiveness. But each religion is basically a language, an approximation of the Mystery. Every one of the languages deserves equal respect and the particular genius of each inspires awe.

While the cosmologies of every great religion seemed to me hopelessly outmoded and merely poetic, the real value of all the religions seemed not their cosmological form but the essential experience of spiritual maturity they espouse—the way they express the matter of coming into wholeness, what Jung called "individuation."

So, while it is true that each religion is the best religion, depending upon who you are, whoever you are and by whatever language you choose, *discover the Mystery*. It is the one worthwhile quest in life!

Particularly interesting to me were the religions of India and the Far East. I was very impressed with the way in which some of the basic insights of these religions had filtered into Western philosophy, particularly in Germany. In this regard, the most sophisticated way of thinking I had ever come across was that of Martin Heidegger. If anyone was dealing with the essence of religion and the truth of Mystery, it was he.

As far as Mystery was concerned, however, I experienced a frustration shared by many growing up in the fifties. There was a kind of banality to life, contributing undoubtedly to the bloodlessness of the theater. Everything was in the same, oppressive order of the day—the boring fifties way of doing things. Being a lover of the primordial and of great drama, I felt frankly out of place, beset with some directionless nostalgia. It seemed that what was vital and interesting had always happened in some other time of place. If you had lived in the time of the Bible, you might be able to see God's backside or experience visions of angels. If you died, you might be able to experience Heaven—or Hell. But in the world I inhabited, there seemed no escape from fatuity. I found myself longing for a scene in which larger-than-life experience was possible.

In 1964, I left America as an expatriate from banality and went to King's College in Cambridge, England, prepared for the possibility that I might not return. It was like stepping into a legend, a magic fairy tale that was nevertheless real. In my requisite academic gowns, I entered into another reality. I walked the medieval courtyards of kings and knights and the baroque corridors of the likes of Newton, Byron, Bertrand Russell and E. M. Forster (who became my friend). It was the happiest time of my life.

I loved the forms, the conventions. It was all theatrical, all taking me far away from that banal American way of doing things. And yet there was another kind of oppression happening at Cambridge. As an American I was free from it, but nevertheless it was numbingly there, in the libraries, the faculty meetings, the parties hosted in the college: The polite mutedness of middle-class English society suppressed every vestige of vitality. It was almost a physical sensation. I could empathize with D. H. Lawrence. Perhaps his spirit had possessed me, for I always found myself barely able to suppress the urge to leap up on the coffee table and yell "FUCK!"

Politely suppressing these urges, I entered Cambridge life with enthusiasm. Having been in American colleges where the extracurricular passion is football, I was delighted to discover that the corresponding passion of Cambridge students was theater! The thespian magic was tangible, quickening, rich. The opening of a new production had the fevered excitement of a Yale-Harvard football game. When my English actor friends spoke Shakespeare, they were not playing at "culture," they were entering into and giving expression to their racial memory. I felt the theater boiling again in my blood.

Of course, in a way it was hopeless. I felt I could never speak English (as opposed to American), never learn to give each consonant its due, never be able to caress each syllable with such exacting authority. But some kindly friends took pity and brought me into a Shakespeare group that toured France, Germany and Switzerland during the long term breaks.

More enchantment! I experienced the magic of small Baroque theaters and the glory of performing before genuinely receptive audiences. My heart still flutters at the memory of a staff being pounded three times on the stage to signal the rising of the curtain, in the tradition of the French stage.

At first, the entire cast would gather backstage to hear whether I would make it through my carefully rehearsed lines without lapsing back into "Umuricun." Finally, however, during my last tour, a special part was created for me in *As You Like It*. Playing a servant, I would come forth at strategic times during the performance and address the audience in their native language, describing who was who and what was going on. This character— a convention in our tours—was enormously popular with the foreign-speaking audiences who otherwise understood little of what was happening. Sometimes I had to play this part in French, and sometimes in German. Improvising was liberally allowed. It gave me a great taste for danger, for stepping out from the proscenium, the script, and the forms into the unknown where audience and performer commune across the proscenium. I lost my taste for any kind of performing that did not provide such excitement.

In time, however, the romantic enhancements of performing in England and during vacations in Europe no longer distracted me from my studies and from my erstwhile discontent with the essential way in which all theater is done. Deep down inside, my being ached at its worthlessness, not just in and of itself but as a symptom of the state of the soul of contemporary humankind.

The essence of my perception of theater is superbly expressed by the great teacher, G.I. Gurdjieff, in his work *Beelzebub's Tales to His Grandson*. As Beelzebub, interstellar adventurer of an enlightened extraterrestrial race, Gurdjieff describes, with an innocent objectivity that voiced my own alienation, the theater of the "sick being," by which he means contemporary Western man devoid of his essence and Origins:

> And these contemporary actors there [on Earth] first reproduce this work themselves alone, without strangers [audience], and they reproduce it until it is exactly as the sick being himself has indicated and as the producer has ordered, and when finally their reproduction proceeds without the participation of their own consciousness and feelings, and these contemporary actors themselves are completely transformed into what are called "living automatons," then and then only, with the help of those among them who have not yet become entirely living automatons—for which reason they later acquire the name of "stage managers"—they do the same thing under their direction, but now in the presence of other ordinary beings assembled in these contemporary theaters.

As polished and pure and technically awesome as I found the British way of doing theater, the essential vacuum I felt at the core of all theater eventually caused my interest to wane...this time, irrevocably. Far more important to me than traditional theatre was my inquiry into the nature of this vacuum, this "sickness," and the Sacred Mystery that had departed. I therefore focused my four and a half years at Cambridge on deciphering the secret language of the phenomenological ontology of Martin Heidegger.

Heidegger brought me to some basics. Most basic of all is that each of us is right here in this existence, and it is the nature of our being to relate with this existence. That is the essence of religion. *Here* is Heaven and a life pursuing it. *Here* also is Hell, and a lifetime avoiding it or dipping into it. Existence itself is the field, the source, and the Mystery. The more we put away inherited and conditioned ways of seeing and being, the more original and satisfying can be our real experience. Life is all about existing and being authentic in our experience of its Mystery.

And behind existence is the most primordial—Being—the source of all law and sense. To know Being is not a matter of learning more about beings, but of *un*learning—becoming more and more primitive in perception. Not savage, but rudimentary. Not barbaric, but essential.

With these insights, and with a growing understanding that the real roots as well as the fulfillment of Heidegger's Way were most likely to be found in the East, I got myself a fine academic appointment as Senior Research Fellow at the Center for Advanced Study in Philosophy at Banaras Hindu University. There, for two and a half years in the milieu of Hinduism, I moved into the awesome sophistication of the religious tradition of India.

One truth I learned in India is that it is possible to achieve an absolutely optimal way of existing, a way of being in Being that corresponds to its truth. There are many words for it in Sanskrit, but in English we call it "enlightenment." This way of being is real, and there are many ways that persons have achieved it, leaving behind a great lore to show others the way. This is the real source of Hinduism, as indeed it is the real source of all great religions and spiritual practice. In each case, someone arrives at this optimal knowing and then, out of the caring that it generates, creates the paths and languages we later come to call religions.

This enlightenment, this optimal way of being, was also, as I had the opportunity to observe, part and parcel of performing art. The great theater, music and dance of India express paths toward enlightenment and the cosmologies in which beings war with the elements to achieve this ultimate state. But even more important is the training of all performers which doubles as a mystical training, or individual *sadhana*, and the process of creating performance which is always a group *sadhana*. All of art serves the process of coming to the Mystery, of enlightenment. No wonder I had found the less ambitious Western theater so boring!

India afforded many glimpses into this state of enlightenment. I saw much evidence that there were those who had actually reached it. I penetrated deeply into the words with which they expressed themselves. And yet I could not say that I had ever seen or touched or knew anyone who had really been there, though my position afforded me access to anyone in India.

What did happen, however, was that I opened up to Being in ways that had been beyond the bounds of a Westerner. This was not only because of my privileged access, but also because of the times—it was the late sixties in India. I befriended some hippies there and began to experiment with psychoactive drugs. A whole world beyond fifties America revealed itself like a magical theater. In every way I opened out beyond what I had known as my identity, my limits or my capacities.

By the time I returned to Europe in 1970 I was in psychological trouble. In the introduction to Richard Wilhelm's translation of the *Secret of the Golden Flower*, Jung explains that it is dangerous for the psyche of a Westerner to penetrate too deeply into the East. The result can only be a deep psychosis which no healthy psyche can assimilate. I am not psychotic, but when I returned to Western Europe it felt as though I were. So great was the gap between who I had become in India and who I had been before and was called upon to be once again, that I often fell over precipices of anxiety that were hardly bearable. I spent almost a year in Zurich at the Jung Institute, carefully monitoring my dreams and heeding their messages to knit myself together into a new synthesis. It was perilous and exciting—a time of great danger and little comprehension.

I believe that Jung's assessment of the dangers of the East-West psychosis was correct, but I feel that he underestimated the actual force by which the world is coming together. East and West *are* becoming one. And it is happening in our generation. It does create a psychosis. *We are in a psychosis*. It is a necessary part of the evolution of the new world consciousness. More often than not, however, it looks as though we are simply falling apart.

In 1970, in Zurich, I was trying to cooperate with the internal forces of integration, to consolidate myself into a new wholeness by going deep into myself on the path of Jung. I found that the Institute was more interested in preserving Jung than continuing in his spirit. In fact, once when I visited Jung's family in the house in Kusnacht where he had lived, I felt his spirit laughing at the sententiousness of it all. But I was glad at last to have moved from my great reading chairs in Cambridge and Banaras and the constructs of my intellect into the soil of my own psyche. And that old passion to discover the arche of the Self found its true soil *my* Self. It was an appropriate welcome into the "me" decade.

In developing my own Western *sadhana*, I monitored with fascination the process by which the East and West within me wove themselves into a new synthesis. Awesome appeared the capacity of the psyche to express this process on so many different levels through its own language of symbols. At certain points in the analysis, symbols would emerge that would offer certain insights that were pertinent at that moment for me, but also universal. It was like watching a garden grow. The spectacle of the Self, the amazing mythos of its unfolding, and the beauty with which it orchestrates itself into disharmonies and harmonies—this was the theater that began to move in my blood once again.

From this experience, I came to understand that growth and integration *happen* as a function of certain insights. And while it is true that those insights happen only in their season, I became fascinated with the prospect of promoting and inducing those integrating moments by means of some sort of experiential form. Now *that* would be theater!

When the theater of my psyche began to emit dream images of dentists on bicycles carrying American flags and bearing down on my teeth to rework them, I realized it was time to end seven years of expatriotism and return to America. But no more East Coast or Middle America for me. I wanted a whole new start, and I knew the place for me to go was California.

There I found the Pacific Ocean daily washing Asia up onto the shores. Everyone seemed to be out on the beaches, sunning their bodies and gathering up Eastern influence, allowing it to inform daring experiments in alternative living. Everything I had been reading, intellectualizing and dreaming about, they were *doing* in California.

In Europe and the East Coast, art and culture were all about the collapse of European values: Nothing works, so let art be the expression of our agonies, our neuroses, our outrage. In contrast to this morbid display was sunny California, especially San Francisco in the early seventies, where every moment was the edge of history, a renaissance of positive alternatives. It was glorious—probably much as it had been in Italy during the Quattrocento. Just as the Italian Renaissance was fed by the assimilation of the Classical periods, so what I called the "Rebellation" in California was fed by the influx of Asian wisdom. It was a grand psychedelic carnival of possibilities and stimuli.

A new world! I had left America, almost a decade before, because I had felt so confined by the American way of doing things. But while I was gone, a whole generation of contemporaries had likewise become fed up with these same routines and with the existential blandness of the fifties ethos. While I was off in far-flung lands trying to reform myself into alternative mentalities, my contemporaries were creating an alternative culture back home in America.

A new kind of theater was one of the results, exploding everywhere in experimentation. I especially noticed and enjoyed it in San Francisco, where the proscenium, that polite division between audience and illusory scene, had fallen by the wayside. There were the Renaissance Faires in which audience and performers alike were part of the scene. There were "People Theater" productions that must have been just like theater a hundred years ago during the Gold Rush. Audiences would get up and shout and throw things at the actors. Performers would invade the audience, destroying its complacency. There was "guerrilla theater" played in the streets or on buses, with the audience comprised of anyone who happened to be around. And of course there were Happenings, those chaotic events in which psychedelics and God-knows-what were the only directors.

As for that other component of theatre which had bored me, mask-making: Acting was everywhere burgeoning into more authentic forms of self-revelation. The Cockettes and Angels of Light were prancing around their cardboard sets, expressing the actual ambiguity of sexual identity and generally "gender-fucking" everyone. Meanwhile, I expressed the theater in my blood by creating different, amazing costumes for my daily wear.

The golden days of California were finished by the second half of the seventies. San Francisco settled down to be just another beautiful city again, and life returned to normal. There were many promises made, great extravagances of expectation sent out into the world, which left some, particularly in Europe, disappointed. Much of the spectacle, ephemeral at best, has disappeared without a trace. The promises of the psychedelic revolution have been largely forgotten or, worse, have gone down the drain into nightmares of drug addiction.

Yet some among those who were there, intrepid existential adventurers, captured real, lasting visions. Through rich excesses we have found our work in life and settled into projects—not so colorful, but no less enthralling—of finding greater and greater substance to our visions. Slowly, these areas of endeavor are making themselves felt throughout the world.

One example is the field of personal growth and therapy. In my first days in California, I became friends with Michael Murphy and Dick Price, the founders of Esalen Institute in Big Sur, the source and nurturing ground of many new and rediscovered technologies of the human potential.

Big Sur was then, and is today, a magical place. From its vantage on towering cliffs along the ocean one can gaze into the infinite expanse of the Pacific and actually see the curvature of the earth and the play of the sun and moon interacting with our planet. Our place in the cosmos seems evident there to the senses, contributing a certain mythic quality to life.

Michael and Dick opened the doors of Esalen for me, into possibilities that exceeded my wildest imaginings. The human potential seemed limitless.

One of the most memorable experiences I have had in theater took place in the first encounter group I attended at Esalen: A woman threw off her persona, opened up, and allowed herself to get behind what she was actually feeling, giving total expression to it. Watching this, I experienced again those long-buried theatrical instincts. This was the warm blood of theater, catharsis, of which masks or acting are but a distant echo.

During that weekend our group was often disturbed by the rowdiness of another workshop that was happening nearby. We kept hearing hilarious laughter. People in silly dress-ups would appear. They were playing children's games on the lawn and wandering around in what seemed to be a wanton state of abandon. The leader of that group subsequently became a dear and time-honored friend. Her name was Marion Saltman, and she lived on a magical ferry-boat in Sausalito which she used to share with Alan Watts.

Marion was one of the pioneers of play therapy. She held encounter groups on her magical boat. Participating in a few, I learned a great deal about regression in the service of higher integration and had a wonderful time to boot. One of the activities was to spend half a day in her phantasmagorical costume collection just dressing up over and over. Like all her techniques, it sounds like frivolity, and certainly looked like it, but the number of sub-personalities I explored was phenomenal. It was a kind of catharsis of hidden identities. We also dressed up and improvised fairy tales much as I had done in children's theater. The delirious playfulness of all this was therapeutic in its own right, but I experienced in myself and saw in others that very profound therapy and vast new levels of integration were happening through this work.

I was also very taken with Gestalt therapy and the use of performance as a way of completing the Self. When we hear the term "whole person," we tend to imagine some absolute quantity or quality that is to be filled out in life. Wholeness is rather the ongoing process of completing ourselves in each situation. Acting out incomplete parts of ourselves for achieving wholeness thus seemed another fascinating possibility for theater.

I made many friendships through Esalen. One of the most important was a former professor of theater from San Francisco State, Paul Rebillot. We sensed a deep connection immediately—one that has certainly fulfilled its promise.

Paul was a true master of theater and Gestalt. He had created a remarkable performing group in San Francisco called the Gestalt Fool. Paul had also discovered Joseph Campbell's work in the sixties while teaching at San Francisco State. He had used *The Hero with a Thousand Faces* as a handbook in training actors and in improvisational work. In his years at Esalen, he created a way to bring the Hero's Journey into a form that could be experienced as a group process.

This was an amazing confluence of paths for me. The Hero's Journey, which had so inspired me as an undergraduate, was here revived in the most vital form of therapeutic process. Paul's version of the Journey has been powerfully effective in enabling health care professionals to bring deeper understanding to their work with persons experiencing schizophrenic episodes, as well as in providing a basis for personal growth on many different levels. In 1974, I had the opportunity to assist Paul in guiding his Hero's Journey process at Esalen. Since that time, I have consulted with him from time to time in the course of developing my own work and have used his process, with my own alterations, as a learning tool for creating my own therapeutic processes.

In the early seventies, word spread among those in the inner mystical circles of Big Sur that a teaching Master from South America named Oscar Ichazo was gathering together an elect group to whom he was passing the real techniques of enlightenment. I found myself packing my bags.

Again I had the overwhelming pleasure of finding that those very things I had been studying abroad in an easy chair were here being actualized. Ichazo had studied all over the world, investigating those religious and mystical traditions that have developed practices and exercises for achieving the state of enlightenment. Much in the manner of Gurdjieff, he had abstracted from these experiences elements and techniques that were objective.

"Objective" here does not mean "verifiable outside of human perception," but rather "universally human." There is a sense in which the subjectivity and being of every human is the same. This "same" human being Ichazo called "the Divine human prototype." What is true of this prototype—its structure (mind, emotion, body), the laws that govern its possible development and evolution, and the techniques that inform and shape that evolution—is said to be objective. This forms the basis of a science of consciousness or a possible technology of optimal human development. For instance, the prototype has an authentic essence and, according to certain laws, it develops an inauthentic ego. To the trained eye, it is always possible to observe whether a person is in essence or ego. There are also laws of process whereby the essence is refined from the dross of ego. When the ego is gone, and the essence alone remains, the optimal conditions for enlightenment are present. The techniques were taken from the mystical schools of the world, abstracted from the religious beliefs in which they may have been contained, and used as objective techniques in the "Work" of the Arica School, which existed to process its members and to train them in the use of these techniques. It was said that "Arica" meant "America" without the "me."

Only a small part of this Work was mental or intellectual. It consisted mostly of bringing the body to its highest and most perfected state as a field for the teachings. The exercises were largely physical, but their teaching was directed toward the heart and the mind. Mystical insights were programmed into the body. It worked rather like timed release programming. Even today, so many years after completing the Work, I find new insights flowering within that I can trace to those hours and hours of repetitive practice.

During the years with Arica, my theatrical instincts were inspired in several significant ways. At about the same time I first heard about Ichazo from John Lilly, I saw *El Topo*, a film by a South American director of Polish descent named Alejandro Jodorowski. It was replete with mystical symbolism, a hero's journey of the quest for enlightenment and the enigmatic teachings of exotic masters. I was awed by this film. Somehow the radical reversion to the body I experienced through Arica training was matched by the radical imagery of the body and the blood in Jodorowski's work.

In fact the connection was stronger that I first suspected. Even as I watched *El Topo*, Jodorowski was making a second film, *The Sacred Moun-*

tain, in conjunction with Ichazo. Many Aricans were taking part in the film, an amazing spectacle of the path to the optimal heights of enlightenment.

I subsequently became friends with Jodorowski. His body-and-the-blood aesthetic, together with his sophisticated commitment to the potential of consciousness, affected me deeply.

There was a group of people in the school, many of whom had worked with Jodorowski, who valued the possibilities of bringing the Arica Work into theatrical expression to make theater and performing technique part and parcel of the project of purifying the essence of ego. We found remarkable ways of dramatizing process. Once, in 1973, during the heyday of the school in New York, we mounted a production in which we dramatized, with conga drum rock and dance, the seduction of the essence by the ego-Monster. It was a sort of objective tribal ritual. I played the Monster and was in a trance throughout the entire performance. The immediacy and vitality of the production blew everybody's mind, including my own. It was a flash of inspiration that was to shape my theatrical instincts for years to come.

In 1975, I made an innocent trip to Asia to see India once again through my new, more "essential" eyes. It proved to be a fateful trip.

As important as the idea of enlightenment was to me, I had not yet encountered anyone—neither in India nor in America—whom I felt to be genuinely enlightened. But during this trip, I found someone that I felt to be most certainly enlightened. In any case, he was so far along the path I had instinctively been following for most of my life that it seemed he was at its disappearing point. His name was Bhagwan Shree Rajneesh.

The day I became his disciple, he amazed me by giving me the name "Veereshwar," a name of Shiva, the god of transformation, that means "Lord of the Heroes!" For ten years from that day, I wore red—the color of vitality.

In his lifetime, Rajneesh was a man of controversy. There were those who claimed that he was the new Messiah. Some that said he was the anti-Christ. There were those who said he was the Buddha, returning to set in motion again the wheel of dharma. There were those who thought him a joke. And there were those that said he was the culminating last of the *Teerthankara,* enlightened Masters of the Jain religion. It seemed to me that history finally decides such matters, and I am quite content to wait.

Rajneesh was called a Master because he was awesomely gifted at expressing the ways and means of the essential experience of religion. He set forth the vision of a new synthesis of East and West, the highest clarity combined with the darkest, wildest Mystery. He was truly a mystic of the blood.

Rajneesh was also a consummate genius of theater. Everything he did, every movement he made, the entire scene he created around him—even the debacles—were theatrical.

Over the years that I visited Rajneesh in India, I learned much about the path to authentic enlightenment and much that bears on performing art as a technique for reaching this ultimate knowing. My previous realization that all art forms are potentially spiritual disciplines was confirmed. Indeed, artists who can overcome the suffering-artist ego have a special proclivity for knowing the Divine. Their technique and craft can be a way of enhancing that proclivity. Through seeing the development of technique as a *sadhana*, a personal mystical Work, artists should forge their form like a Zen arrow, perfectly aimed towards its target—the One.

Rajneesh presented meditation as pure repose in consciousness. It is a non-volitional state in which mind (the primary volitional activity) is stilled. What remains is Divine and, if simply followed, can lead to the ultimate knowing. In our time, we cannot even approach this state because our minds are insane and we are totally identified with them—especially in the West. This insanity, compacted with centuries of repressed feeling and sexual energy, has to be thrown off, catharted. In the practice of catharsis we can learn how to let go, a practice that is essential for meditation. Once we have thrown off our madness, the real quietude of meditation can occur. Then we can learn to surrender into those realities—those Origins—that are essential to our real consciousness.

Sex, anger and the catharsis of strong emotion are very dynamic aspects to which it is relatively easy to learn to surrender. Music, love, the presence of a spiritual Master are more subtle emissions to which we may surrender. Any technique that throws us into a non-volitional state serves our capacity for meditation, and true meditation serves our capacity to know the Divine. If we become quite surrendered in improvisation, we can just turn off our control and allow performance to happen. As such, improvisation is also a technique for meditation.

Discovering meditation is all about learning how to surrender and how to let go of resistance. Learning about the Divine is the same discipline, following the gentle persuasion of the inner being toward enlightenment. Hence the teaching of surrender and resistance is essential to spiritual instruction.

Through Rajneesh I also came to realize that creativity is the highest form of worship. To be creative is to praise the Creator and to commune with it. Hence the act of creation is a kind of offering, and the more our creative work is centered in the disposition of offering, the closer we come to communion with the Divine.

On one of my trips to India I went with my beloved to Bali. One night, we went to a production of the Ramayana that was held in a temple. I do not know whether it was because I was in love, or because of the full moon or because I was able to fall completely under the spell of the gamalan music, but I had an experience of theater that changed me profoundly.

The Ramayana is a simple love story of a hero and heroine, separated by a monster and brought together with the help of a monkey god. But what happened there at the entrance to the temple somehow entered me and penetrated into the core of my own unconscious symbology. There was no proscenium here; the entrance to the temple was the entrance to my own psyche. There were no masks here; the characters were the living symbols of my innermost parts, so that the separation of masculine and feminine, and its blissful reunion at the culmination, actually happened within me, within my spirit, within my own psyche.

This experience of an outer theatrical event doubling itself within my deepest being gave me my first glimpse of theater in its primordial form. In every tradition, drama and theater originated as a manifestation of religious ritual which was intended to affect its audience in just the way I had been affected. The dramatized action was to become one with the innermost movements of the psyche, so that the inner psyche of the audience and the ritual action at the temple's entrance were one and the same.

This is where theater came from. This healing ritual was the forgotten essence, the true primeval origin of performing art.

In the second half of the seventies, between extended visits to India and the Ashram in Poona, I began experimenting more and more with theatrical techniques in therapy and beyond. I completed a Ph.D. in transpersonal psychology, specializing in individual and group process, and expanded my own work in individual hands-on therapy and group workshops, combining Jungian and Arican Work and meditation techniques of all kinds with performance expression.

This growing enthusiasm for therapy was fired by a deepening realization that creativity, the most authentic form of worship, and expression are two essential, even holy aspects of human nature which, when activated, have an intrinsically healing effect. Moreover, through creative expression and analysis of the works created, Self-awareness happens and Self-acceptance, even Self-love, is generated. These two, awareness and Self-love, are the authentic healing elements in therapy and the basis of any *sadhana* which affords psychological growth and well-being. They are also the equivalents, in transpersonal psychology, of authentic worship.

In my enthusiasm for this form of therapy, I became involved with a consortium of expressive arts therapists. We formed the Center for Transpersonal and Expressive Arts Therapies in Los Angeles, which promoted and practiced it. Through this TEAT Program, we trained therapists in all forms of therapeutic techniques employing the expressive arts.

Over time, the streams of interest in my life came together and began flowing in stronger and stronger channels. As my therapeutic work expanded and progressed, and as I became more and more interested in the artistic possibilities in my work, I found myself reversing the trend away from art to science. I began putting together little shows and plays here and there. I found myself falling deeper and deeper into places within myself where philosophy, mythology, therapy and performing art came together.

One day in 1980, shortly after I turned forty, I was in the mountains of California. I had a clear impulse from within to bring together all these strands that flow through my veins into one form, one process. The result was a new conception of performing art. But what would I call it?

In the late seventies, I had been in Poona when Rajneesh delivered a series of lectures on the *Diamond Sutras* of Gautam Buddha. He began the first lecture with the following salutation: "My beloved Bodhisattvas, I salute you." Two and a half millenia ago, the Buddha had delivered the Diamond Sutras, in which he explained to his disciples that the existential righteousness set forth by his teaching would, in 2,500 years, degenerate and have to be revived. It was the Bodhisattvas, true disciples of the righteouness, who would regenerate the true Way. This, Rajneesh said, was to be the work of his disciples. The lectures were an awesome inspiration to rise to our utmost in service to the highest. As my new conception of performance began to take shape, I remembered these words about the Bodhisattva and the regeneration of existential righteousness. It therefore seemed appropriate to call this new conception of performance "Bodhisattva Arts," and it seemed right to dedicate my love and my energy to it as such for several years after.

My understanding of the mission behind the Bodhisattva was subsequently broadened and deepened, and its direction greatly clarified, by extended excursions to Bali. My experience of the *Ramayana*, that primordial glimpse of the sacred moment of ritual performance, beckoned me back to that paradisical isle enchanted by living gods. With each visit has come ever-deeper initiation into the Origins and nature of sacred performing arts, and new inspirations regarding their possibility in guiding the future of humankind. It is no accident that the patron deity of Bali is *Sangyang Witi*, the god of inspiration.

On Bali, one can sense and witness the moment—lost to the rest of the world—when performance emerged as a vital expression of a living spiritual tradition. If one has the good fortune to be allowed to partake in the mysteries of trance performing, it is possible to experience the most vivid connection between the performance and the Divine. In this archaic performing mode, the performer loses all self-possession and becomes possessed by the spirit.

I was once invited into the holy of holies of the temple of Champuan to witness the appearance of seven divine spirits presenting themselves through two pre-pubescent girls in a trance. The medium of transmission was sacred masks that had been carved four hundred years ago by a mask-maker, himself possessed by the divinities. First, the girls were put into their trance. Then, one by one, a mask was placed on each girl in turn and the corresponding divinity would enter our presence through her dance. The spirits were tangibly present in unspeakable grace and loveliness.

This is not to be dismissed as mere hocus-pocus. It is the displacement of the mask of the ego and the arrival of the divinity. Trance is similar to catharsis in which the *persona* disappears and the extremity of feeling and situation take over, but trance is deeper. Catharsis is personal; trance performance is trans-personal. Yet they both come out of the same kind of surrender, the same let-go that I had discovered through the dynamic meditations of Rajneesh, the same displacement of the small self for the great Self, the Origins. This is the same phenomenon as the speaking of the Pythian oracle at Delphi, the same as the "channeling" phenomenon (when it is authentic) that was so popular in some circles during the eighties. But it is not merely "esoteric"—it is basic, fundamental. It exposes at once a dangerous blind spot in our modern consciousness and the possibility of a kind of performing art that is a vehicle for the Mystery, the Divine: *sacred* performing art in which the Origins themselves can speak.

For years, like a blind man, I had been groping for this sense of performance, discontent with the art of mere technique and control, fascinated with improvisation, the reality of true catharsis, the notion of personal and technical skill which allows one to step aside for the Divine within—all of this fired my enthusiasm to rediscover and bring into my performing arts conception a contemporary form of performance expression in which the Divine Human Prototype, the Sacred, could be given its voice. I have come to call this "entheotic" performing.

But the god of inspiration did not stop with these remarkable initiations into the Origins of sacred performing art. He also inspired a whole new vision for the future.

In 1983, shortly after arriving in Bali, new-found friends directed us toward the great volcano, Batur. There, we were told, is a center for the creation of an efficacious art of the future. Its visionary octogenarian director is Professor Sultan Takdir Alisjahbana, renowned poet and philosopher, Chairman of the Indonesian Academy of Arts and President of the National University. He is known as the "father of the Indonesian language" because, throughout most of this century, he spearheaded the effort to transform the Malaysian language into *Bahasa Indonesia*, a complete modern language which now unites into one nation all of the 350 or so diverse island cultures of the Indonesian archipelago. In recent years, the professor has turned his attention to the arts as an international language that can unify the world.

Professor Alisjahbana explained his work to me. The arts, he believes, have degenerated into products of anarchistic individualism or mere commercial interest. He thus created, on Bali, the Toyabungkah Center and the World Association for Art and the Future, in order to influence artists to contribute to a future in which the dilemmas that beset the world will come to a new equilibrium. Science may make a great contribution because it is objective and quantitative, allowing great manipulation through technology, but the arts, through their suggestive and evocative power, touch the heart and fertilize the imagination and intuition to give the human mind motivation and direction for shaping the future.

As the professor and I became fast friends, my growing understanding of the source of sacred performing art met with a sophistication and noble concern for the future. He gave me courage as an artist to take responsibility for the future. He inspired me to revise my understanding of what a Bodhisattva artist really is: One who has a vision of wholeness grounded in the Origins and can project this vision to make the world whole.

The entire context of my quest took a change. The light of the past began to illuminate the way of the future. The most archaic became the hope for the new. The quest for the source of performance became the inspiration to create a performing art for the future.

My path through four decades has sometimes seemed aimless and arbitrary. Actually, the fifties were a time to partake of the traditions of performance and to grow weary with its essential pent-up banality. In the sixties, the dam broke in an explosion of new values and "far-out" possibilities. The seventies were a time to explore "me," self-realization through true individual *sadhana* and real mysticism. The eighties—the years of the antithetical Reagan ethos—were a time to go underground for deep penetration into the real substance behind these possibilities, synthesizing, tightening.

Clearly, whatever is going to serve man in the future will be an obeisance in kind to what man has always been in his essence. Sacred performing art is a way of returning to the essence, an initiation by which the Origins bring us back to the Source. It is only be reckoning with these Origins that humankind can rightly center its thrust into the future.

On the basis of this realization and because, on a practical level, the word "Bodhisattva" was too esoteric a concept for a Western name and difficult to pronounce, I changed the name of this work to ORIGINS in the mid-eighties. It designates the work as an attempt to return to the origins of performing arts and give expression through performance to the Origins of Being itself.

My work with Bodhisattva Arts and ORIGINS has taken me all over the world. Wherever I go there are always some people, a handful, who—as if with tremendous impetus from the archaic past—understand intrinsically what the Work is. It is as though such people had already thought of it, or already knew what it is from within their own artistic and spiritual intuition. In ORIGINS we speak of a silver cord by which such people are joined with us. They are the beloved.

To those already connected by the silver cord, to those who already understand, and to those who would know more—this work is dedicated.

Introduction:
Performance and the Sacred

It is the time of the gods that have fled
and the gods that have not yet come.

These lines from the poetry of the German Romantic, Friedrich Hoelderlin, seem to me the most concise and profound utterance about this, our time in history. Certainly they were for Martin Heidegger, who wrote extensively about them. They reveal what Heidegger calls "the time of the double-not": the old gods are no longer with us, and the new gods have not yet arrived.

It is the time of the gods that have fled.

For 2,500 years, the Sacred has been housed in the temples of the great religions. But the time of the great religions is over.

As belief structures, religions contradict each other. The very existence of so many religions in our world makes the absolute truth of any one of them unacceptable to anyone with real discrimination. The contradictions among the Western religions are exacerbated by the incursion of the religious traditions from the East. The extreme sophistication of these traditions obviates the hegemony of any one religion that does not in some way circumscribe all others. The fragmentation from this contradiction at this time makes exclusive religious belief unacceptable to intelligence.

Untenable is the divisiveness in the world created through religious fundamentalism. Each believer takes his religion to be the one and only that is correct and appropriate. Throughout history more blood has been spilt over religious beliefs than for any other single reason. The existential ambiguities and uncertainties of our time propel the sects of the world into even more virulent fanaticism, increasing the world problems created by fundamentalism.

Equally dysfunctional is the generation of stringent ideals. Religious ideals are the basis of any religious ethos. Stringent ideals rob people of their individuality. Over time, this frustrated individuality creates collective rage and the destruction of the very institutions that impose those ideals.

Moreover, the moral ideals of one religion contradict the ideals of another. This generates national and cultural differences that become powerfully competitive.

"God is dead!" This was the cry of a madman in a poem written by Friedrich Nietzsche a hundred years ago. What he meant is that we have evolved a view of reality that precludes God. Knowledge has supplanted belief as the basis for existence. Look at the college curriculum! Everything is explainable in physical, economic, historical, or psychological terms. Who needs the gods? Who needs God?

And yet...

It is the time of ... the gods that have not yet come.

The metaphors of the past have collapsed, but the sacred laws of Being and existence are not dead. They have not disappeared into the void. The universe is not chaotic, without form or direction. Existence and Being are not lawless. My own teachers—Heidegger, Jung, Ichazo, Gurdjieff and Rajneesh—prophets all, have revealed in different ways our common ground in sacred Being.

A new view of the Sacred is coming, a new paradigm—not of the ideal, but of the whole. The gods are *there*. It is only that they have been obscured by the ambiguities and blindness of our time and cannot therefore be named.

Because the gods have no name, we behave as though they do not exist. Because "God is dead," we live in a kind of existential anarchy. Drunken with godlessness, we err, wandering in meaninglessness, destroying our environment. This erring is itself evidence that we have missed the gods. We have lost our roots in Being. We are destroying our planet. We are bereft.

The time of the truth that has fled and the truth that has not yet come is a time of powerful and cataclysmic cultural change, of great danger. Yet the double-not is, in its own way, a positive, for this spiritual and religious vacuum is rich in possibilities. The prophets are telling us to return to authenticity, to who we are, to nature within and without, to Mother Earth— to the sacred Origins. It is the exciting and creative circumstance in which life in our time is to be understood. And yet, as a basic existential context, the double-not reveals our basic existential need.

It is the place of authentic religion to answer the basic existential need of humankind. Religion forms the way in which man abides in his Being. It determines whether he is at home or not. Living in the time of the double-not means that we are there in existence, but no longer at home.

Through authentic art, man establishes and registers his *present* relationship to existence. Art has a special sensitivity to its times. It is not imposed, not the product of a collective agreement as is religion. It is the expression of individual sense and sensibility with regard to existence. If I am living in a religious time, the religion defines my relationship to existence. If I am an artist living in a time when *the* religion is no more, it falls to my art to define my relationship to existence.

Therefore, in the last two hundred years, art has been called upon to respond to the spiritual needs of man. The time of the double-not defines the place of art and also the place of the artist.

Performance is the art form that has been most primordially associated with religions the world over. As the outgrowth of religious ritual, performance is the primary form of communion between the Sacred and the community. For this reason the performing arts are in a particularly sensitive circumstance in the time of the double-not.

We come then to a central question: What is the role of performing art in the time of the gods that have fled and the gods that have not yet arrived?

The Pursuit of the Origins

Times of change in history produce insecurity. In such critical times, people look backward to find a stable base. The changes brought about by liberal policies, for instance, create an instability which causes us to elect officials who call for a return to values from the past. The more basic the changes, the more remote the past into which we are drawn. In the fourteenth century, the Middle Ages were at an end. It did not suffice to become more conservatively feudal. Rather, it was necessary to return to ancient Greece and Rome for inspiration. Thus the Renaissance.

The new age that will emerge from the time of the double-not represents a change of major proportions. It is perhaps the pivotal change in the history of humankind. Thus our attraction is to the first beginnings, the *arche*. We see this in all areas of human endeavor.

In the area of religious belief, this reversion is apparent in fundamentalism. We have seen how the insecurity of the double-not is generating a new wave of sectarian fanaticism the world over. But religious fundamentalism will not serve in the long run because the roots of the problem are deeper. The true Origins are to be found in the oneness of humankind, not the differences. The reaction in fundamentalism is towards the origins of the sect, not towards the true *arche*, the one. It is divisive in the world—contributing to conflicts that are no longer functional. The archaic revival has to return to the real Origins.

Everywhere in systematic inquiry there is the search for the basic universals. In science there is the quest for the bases of physical being, the beginnings of the universe and the planet. In the cultural sciences there is anthropology, which inquires into the intrinsic order of indigenous man and his communities for the lost art of living in harmony with nature.

The inquiries concerned with the Sacred, with the spirit of man and his existence, are psychology, philosophy, and comparative religion. In psychology we pursue the elements of behavior. In psychoanalytic theory, there is the uncovering of basic instincts and laws by which the psyche operates. Analytic psychology probes into the sources of human experience and development, the archetypes of the collective unconscious of humankind.

In philosophy there is the attempt to revert to the Origins in Phenomenology, the return to original experience itself beyond what is construed by our conditioned minds. Heidegger brought this inquiry into a basic "destruction" of our whole "metaphysical" way of understanding things and construing reality in favor of a return to Being as it primordially shows itself. The Origins are the first manifesting of every now.

The pursuit of the Sacred led to the inquiry into the emanation of the gods that have fled. The study of comparative religions seeks the commonalities behind all religions. Here the Origins are the authentic, sacred ground of Being that is expressed in the language of the world religions.

The wide-ranging, non-traditional spiritual movements in the seventies and eighties sought the Source with renewed vigor. How to understand and gain access to the ancient ones? What is the universal truth from which we all come? What authentically belongs to the one human being, the divine human prototype? And how, therefore, is it appropriate to be?

In general, the archaic revival is a return to nature. This has been part of the quest of the artist and the scientist in the West since the beginning of the Romantic Period at the close of the eighteenth century. But the return to nature today has an urgency to it that is far greater than the sentimental longings of most nineteenth-century thinkers. The ecological challenge, which exists at a physical, psychological and spiritual level, has made the realignment with nature a matter of planetary life or death. The question of survival comes to this: What is the center of nature, both physically and spiritually, around which it organizes itself so that each aspect has its place, each tendency is balanced?

All of these questions into the center of nature and of man are probes— desperate fumbling for the Sacred in the time of the no-more and the not-yet.

Performing Art and the Sacred

Truly, the existential need to touch into the authentic Origins is vital to the human race. Nothing but the real thing will do. The yearning and disease of the human soul is too great. The ecological threat too real.

The arts, particularly the performing arts, have a strategic role in all of this. In a certain sense, all art expresses this state of being. Every instance of performing art can be related to it. But the performing arts as we know them today are largely a form of distraction, a retreat into the confines of mere form, a shirking of responsibility. They are devoid of the Sacred and are therefore deeply profane.

At the most base level, the profane performing arts are conceived as an industry. "Producing" and "packaging" performances, including film and television, is a major world industry. As such, the main objective and concern is *what will sell*. And the result, in a real sense, is that the "entertainment industry" *has* taken over the role of religion, but in a negative sense, as understood by Karl Marx when he described religion as the "opiate of the people." The performing arts, debased into mere entertainment, are a fundamental form of escapism. This is the antithesis of their original function.

Somewhat further up the scale of "culture" are performances that function as a kind of living museum. Their purpose is to preserve the great traditions and institutions of performance in music, theater, opera and dance. The emphasis is placed on excellent *re-creation* of great works from the past. In this role as "mere culture" the performing arts have a function, to provide traditional forms of beauty for the ennoblement of cultural experience. They subtly seduce us into believing that we have a currently viable human identity because others have had one in the past.

Beyond this is performing art that represents "highest culture." What happens here is largely a retreat of the artist into the form. Performing is for other performers and for connoisseurs of the art. Such work is usually too obscure and recondite for anyone else to be interested. This is art for art's sake.

Each of these kinds of performing art certainly has its own kind of legitimacy. They are all, in their own way, pleasing. The industry provides entertaining distraction. The museum art sustains "culture." Art for art's sake serves the artists and the arts. In a larger sense, the vapidity of spirit in these kinds of performing art *express* the time of the double-not. Taken together, they are at least symptomatic of that time. But none of them addresses the responsibility of performing art to the true existential need of our time. None of them serves the original function of performing: to heal by bringing the community in touch with the Sacred.

After some years of experimentation in the performing arts, I have come to understand this cultural context as it corresponds to my own personal sense of emptiness, that which set me on my quest in the first place and kept me on it. I created ORIGINS as a program for addressing these fundamental issues. I see it as the missing link between performing art and the Sacred in the time of the double-not.

This book explores in depth the ORIGINS program as a concrete basis for considering two fundamental questions:

• Who is the holy performer?
• What is Sacred Performance?

The Holy Performer

We know a great deal about profane performers. Gossip, scandal and personality magazines saturate us with every detail of their lives. They are those colorful personalities—with artistic temperaments all—who have successfully survived the compromise with their original spiritual inspiration in an essentially commercial activity. Their egos are outrageous—the stuff of legend! Their appetite for fame, glory and center stage is insatiable—a public joke.

I believe that the ego of the profane performer is insatiable because he has to survive in a performance mode which does not really nourish the deep instinctive inspiration that moves him on the most basic level. His work is not an authentic response to true existential need—either his own need or the need of the society. It is like someone who has a chronic appetite for junk food because his body has never known real nourishment.

By contrast, the holy performer is close to the Origins of performing art. His work is an authentic confrontation with those Origins and, through them, with himself. His path is an ongoing purification of his ego in the face of the awesome truths whose vehicle he strives to become. This is the spiritual path that is his life work, for he is in essence a mystic.

ORIGINS is a training which defines the work of the performer in the context of a *sadhana*, a basic spiritual or mystical discipline. By tracing the steps of the performer through this Process, we can answer some basic questions. What is holiness? What is the journey of the performer to become holy? In what way does he have to confront the Origins? What is his spiritual path? And what is his work?

Sacred Performing Art

There have been and are artists working in the area of sacred performing art. The giant of the nineteenth century was Richard Wagner. We have much to learn from his genius as well as his excesses. In this century there is Jerzy Grotowski and Peter Brook in theater. Alejandro Jodorowski and Ingmar Bergman have produced stunning works in film. But for the most part, performing art long ago outgrew and abandoned its original sacred function. Clearly, however, if performing art is going to serve humankind in this time of existential need, there must be an obeisance in kind to what man has always been in his essence—the Origins.

Performing art that does not reach intuitively into the emerging world religion does not address the truth of our time—the yearning of the human soul for the center of existence and nature. Performing art that does not address this spirit is in the end irrelevant, mere escapism. And its refusal to address this need contributes to the danger of survival.

Sacred performance is and always has been a way of returning to the essence, an initiation by which the community is brought back to its Source. As such, sacred performance addresses the present. But by virtue of the depths to which it penetrates and the definitions it generates, it also addresses the future. It shapes and envisions that which is to be. It forms the mentality of the future.

ORIGINS is a program which creates a form of performance that can be authentically sacred. By tracing the creation of works in the ORIGINS Process, we can answer some basic questions. What is the Sacred? What does sacred performing art proceed from? What are the essential ingredients? And what is the responsibility of sacred performance in the creation of the future of humankind?

The ORIGINS Process

There are certain seminal books that are milestones in the journey of the mind. Such a book for me was *The Birth of Tragedy*, by Friedrich Nietzsche. It is a brilliant and powerful analysis of human existence, in the form of a description of the nature of Greek tragedy. Perhaps more than any other work, this masterpiece revealed to me the true core of my interest in the performing arts. The psychology that it sets forth will provide a basis for understanding the ORIGINS Process.

In ancient Greece, Apollo, Charioteer of the Sun, was the god of restraint, harmony and measure, embodied in classical sculpture and architecture. The ambisexual Dionysus was the wild, archaic mystery expressed in the frenzies of Dionysian music and revels. The birth of Greek tragedy out of the rites of Dionysus was for Nietzsche a triumph of Apollonian form, "the sublime as the artistic conquest of the horrible." Nietzsche lauded the Greeks for creating a new order of beauty by giving form to terrors of nature and history and creating tragedies in which life in all its vicissitudes was affirmed.

But there were implications for Nietzsche far beyond this historical thesis. The character of Western man was determined by these two gods. Apollo is logic, light, reason, the dream, the principle of individuation—the ideal. He is the Spirit. Dionysus is the irrational, the unconscious, music. He is the dark impulses of the Mothers of Being, embassies of the Origins. The split between these two realities has created a psychic schism which has determined the nature of our civilization. With the occurrence of Christianity, the ethos of Apollo was identified with the way of Christ, and Dionysus was relegated to the dark, his attendant satyrs becoming the prototype of the devil: Apollo and Dionysus, Christ and Satan, Good and Evil.

There was something wrong in this polarization and degeneration into mere moral terms. The Greeks honored both gods in kind, and Nietzsche's thesis is that Greek tragedy represented a tense synthesis of Dionysian energy and Apollonian form. With the Christian prejudice, however, the vitality of the Mothers of Being was relegated to the red darkness. And darkness to evil. This is the source of the so-called white man's disease, the root of the neurosis of modern Western man.

Without the grounding, energy, and wisdom of the Origins, man is out of balance. Nietzsche considered the Greek ideal of the Olympians to be a flight from the terrors and richness of existence. The Christian tradition took this flight even further afield. In a sense, the West has been trying to right itself from this imbalance since the time of the Romantics. The Apollonian-Christian ideal had reigned like a tyrant over the West, and, for the last two hundred years, the dark, irrational forces of the Mothers have been avenging themselves. The chaos of our time is a reaction of a culture repressed by the ideal. Reality is seeking a new order.

This struggle takes on new dimensions with the light from the East. In our generation the preeminent truths of Eastern thought are being received for the first time with real comprehension. The East—particularly the traditions originating in India and China—provides a view of existence which does not rest upon the split between the Apollonian and the Dionysian that has characterized the West. There is another, higher way, in which spirit and matter, soul and body, rational and irrational, conscious and unconscious are one. The division is not absolute or, for that matter, real. We all somehow know this in our gut. There is ONE—the true Origins—and it is obscured by the illusion of division. The new world order has to do not with the ideal, but with the total. Not with the triumph of good over evil, but with the ascendancy of the whole over the divisiveness of all dualities, including good and evil.

In myself, I worship with my aspirations at the shrine of Apollo, but in my nature, I am a passionate devotee of Dionysus, because *there* is my vitality. Early in life, before I can even remember, I made a commitment to honor the wild horses of my nature, no matter what the cost. All of my internal and external life work has been involved with making a new kind of synthesis. I believe that everyone of us who is really alive is somehow or other implicated in this transition. It is the force of history.

The performance stage is a scene where the vital essence of life can be projected. As a young man, already a veteran of professional theater, I felt disappointment and frustration at a bloodless theater in a culture that was spiritually and sexually repressed. These feelings are poignantly expressed by Karl Maria von Rilke in the *Duino Elegies IV*, where he describes the professional dancer as the image of modern man:

... How gracefully he moves!
And yet he is disguised, a dressed-up philistine,
who will come home soon, entering through the kitchen.
I cannot bear these masks, half-filled with life.

I felt that the culture was entirely too unbalanced in favor of the
Apollonian. It had lost its energy substance, the vitality of the Dionysian. It
is precisely this denatured element—the Origins—that has to be restored to
its rightful place, but not in the form of rock and rape; it has to be *resyn-
thesized* with the Apollonian. And then a new vision, a wholistic, world vision
has to arise which transcends all dichotomies.

And this is the project: *to restore the Dionysian to its pre-eminence; to find
the pure balance of the Apollonian and the Dionysian; and to clarify the higher
synthesis by which they are one.* This is the process of the unfolding of a new
world culture. It is the heart of therapy, religion, philosophy and art. Any
authentic myth of our time must of necessity deal with this transformation.

The word "bodhisattva" is a Buddhist term for an enlightened one who
remains in the world to show others the way. I see the Bodhisattva of our time
as the potential for a higher synthesis of the Apollonian and the Dionysian—
one made possible by the synthesis of East and West. As a principle, this
possibility lives in all of us as the seed of Self-realization, the new, total human
potential.

The innovative conception of performance set forth here gives expression to this principle as it lives in our time. Through the vision of the
performing artist, this Bodhisattva quickens the view of the coming planetary
human being, expressing the highest possibilities for humankind in this
singular, yet threatening axis of history. The Bodhisattva is the hope for a
whole man who can shape a whole planet. It was for this reason that the
Process now called ORIGINS was first named "Bodhisattva Arts." It was intended as an open laboratory in which the alchemy of this transformation can
be worked out and dramatized into living mythology, an authentic investi-
gation into the unnamed gods of our time.

ORIGINS

The ORIGINS Process is a new way of creating performance. It is a process of
individual development that takes place in a group which may consist of five
to twenty-five participants. It is an intense training in four steps that may be

condensed into a minimum of five full days or extended to a maximum of two months. The Process involves very deep self-exploration and expression through what I call archetypal psychodrama, and it ends in a production which gives expression to the group's transformational process.

There are two separate trainings which follow the same four stages. One of them is based on the archetypal form of the Hero's Journey. The other is based on the archetypal form of the Love Story. These trainings differ in substance, but their form, the ORIGINS Process, remains the same. The four stages are as follows.

Stage I: CHAOS

The performers are brought to a point of catharsis where they can give expression, beyond inhibition, to their most primal sources. This basic skill builds the internal confidence of the performer to experience the original Self and give expression to it before an audience without censorship or design.

Stage II: DREAM

The archetypal plot form (either the Hero's Journey or the Love Story) is introduced and its psychological significance and power is explored. Each participant experiences and performs himself through his version of each character in the archetype. The participant then acts out his own Dream, his version of the plot form, playing the several characters. Each of these psychodramatized Dreams is then analyzed by the group. The participant is transformed by the power of the archetype and comes to an understanding of how the Self reveals itself through the plot form.

Stage III: MYTH

The group now creates a version of the archetypal plot form which expresses its common Self, its "Myth." The performers create a story line and a "score" with commonly agreed upon cues, basic actions, and lines. Parts are taken according to the specific expressive talents and needs of each participant. The Myth is then performed improvisationally before an audience which may participate in some form or another.

Stage IV: RITUAL

The performance of the Myth, modified by the feedback from the audience, is used as the prototype for a complete score or script which is mounted into a full-scale production and performed as a ritual offering to five essentials: the highest development of consciousness, the archetypal plot form, the Spirit of Nature, the power of the Monster, and all of humanity.

The purpose of the first half of the training (the first two Stages) is to transform the individual. The first Stage, CHAOS, restores, through deep cathartic work, the Dionysian energy to the performer. In the second Stage, the DREAM, the Apollonian aspect is introduced. These two Stages together provide the possibility for the transformation of the performer through experiential and existential discovery of the Origins—the unnameable gods manifest within each human universe. Through this dramatic confrontation a new vision of wholeness, the Bodhisattva, can come into being.

The purpose of the second half of the training is to discover the myth of the group and create from it a ritual to transform the community. In the third Stage, the MYTH, the group creates together a story that expresses their collective transformation, which they subsequently dramatize and present as a production in Stage IV, the RITUAL.

Since 1980 an ORIGINS Production Company has existed in various forms with the purpose of presenting these performances to the public. The productions have been greatly varied in form and highly experimental in nature. They often take place in unusual settings, both inside and outside.

Participants in the productions are, by and large, obliged to complete both the Hero's Journey and the Love Story Training in order to master the unique technique of performing that is often, but not always, characteristic of ORIGINS productions. "Entheotic performing" is the name given to acting, singing or dancing whose basic content is not pre-set or composed, but rather created in the moment. The word is taken from the Greek word from which the English "enthusiasm" is derived. *En-theos* means "entered and possessed by the god." It is the basic form of the verb used to describe the entering of the Delphic Oracle by the god Apollo. Entheotic performing is the technique of channelling the unnameable gods.

ORIGINS is a new and yet very ancient conception of sacred performance. It returns the blood back into the art. In one process, it contains a therapeutic and personal growth method, an artistic conception, and a religious form.

• It is a *therapy and personal growth program* in which participants undergo a transformation which is profoundly healing and expanding and discover a path of Self-realization which is at the same time an artistic discipline. The result of the Process is a production which is a Ritual of transformation for the audience.

• ORIGINS is an *artistic conception.* The actual production may be a ballet, a film, an opera, a stage play, or something that has no precedent at all. The form can vary enormously, because the Process actually generates only a content. It is an objective art form which reveals the nature of the Self and allows it to be expressed through a genuine mythology. It is an artistic vision of optimal human development.

• ORIGINS is a *religious form* in that it explores the fundamental relationship of man to existence. It is a religion that is not antagonistic to any Religion, but absolutely complementary. It is a method for clarifying the nature of evil and of transmuting it. It is a form, not involving belief, which produces mystical insight. The form is an expression of God as the experience of wholeness.

Before presenting each Stage of the ORIGINS Process in detail, here are some basic elements and aspects that need to be understood.

The Group

There is nothing more precious than the individual. The lonely interface between the conscious self and our existence is the true field of religion. This is where each of us meets God.

Nevertheless, in the ORIGINS Process, the group is the most important entity. It is the vehicle by which individuals may be transformed. It grounds all activity and change. It is the base from which individuals can safely make flights into the unknown. The dynamic genius of the group working in unity will create a mythical medium through which the Divine *may* speak. And finally it is the level of the group by virtue of which the Divine *will* speak.

During the years in which I have been developing the ORIGINS Process, I have worked with many kinds of special groups: neurotics, people variously interested in self-development, women, gays, clowns, Aricans, Rajneesh disciples, persons with AIDS, dancers, singers, actors and performers of all kinds. The productions have been equally diverse. Whatever the production requires seems to be miraculously available in each group. It doesn't seem to matter how it is formed. I have often sat before a group in the opening exercises and wondered how a production could possibly come together with such a motley assortment, but the miracle is that each group forms itself into a unity and finds within itself everything and everyone that is needed.

The group constitutes a world of its own. In the sixties, workshops became an institution in their own right. I have often thought about this institution. In part it is a response to the fact that the greater world, which used to be made up of thousands of cultures, is rapidly becoming one. The security and community of small, autonomous cultural groups has been lost. The workshop creates a situation in which this autonomy is recreated.

The workshop context is a setting for playing with reality, for examining behavior by reordering, exaggerating, fragmenting and recombining reality. In the ORIGINS Process, the group becomes a sort of religious order. In this protected context, a sublanguage and subculture emerge in which rational, arational and irrational behavior exist in a balance.

The evolution of the group in the ORIGINS training is one of the most interesting aspects of the entire experience. From my point of view it is an *ad hoc* society organizing itself slowly into a new order through the introduction of a structure of religious belief. As the Process proceeds, the Self-experience of many diverse individuals gets redefined and reorganized. Each individual comes into a new Self-understanding and vocabulary which he shares in common with others. The group vocabulary takes on the aspect of a religion. It is a true religion, but its specific form is always ephemeral.

This "tribal" situation is imposed on the group at the first meeting by a very specific device. The group members are shown how to form themselves into a perfect circle. They are told that the level of the group is always evidenced by its capacity at each meeting to sit in such a perfect circle. When the circle becomes uneven, the group is reminded about its level. Attention to this detail is one of the ways that group unity is built up and maintained. This unity is essential as it grounds all activity and change.

Within this tribal circle, a great adventure is to take place in which each person is unique and simultaneously part of a whole. A new tribal cosmology is going to evolve.

My Role in the Training

When those who are unfamiliar with my work ask me what I do, I am always at a loss for words. I have often deliberated over this quandary. What to say? Group leader? Therapist? Teacher? Director? Producer? All of these say something, but they describe very poorly the actual function that I serve in this Work.

In a sense I see my function as something like a shaman, a holy man. Finding myself in a world of collapsed metaphors where religion and theater no longer serve real existential need, I have roamed the world and sought within and without the vital essence in order to create a kind of practical religious exercise, an exercise whose truth and form remain the same but whose specific manifestation changes constantly. Like the shaman, I have undergone a personal journey to discover a new way of organizing experience that can be presented to others. It is a healing journey, one that salves the soul and sets it upon the path of true growth.

In the actual progress of the group, I function as the leader. Here my work is to employ the carefully ordered techniques I have devised in order to free performers into their full creative power and to monitor the basic device of the Process, the archetypal plot form.

As the training progresses, I function in other capacities. In the earlier stages of the Process, developed largely in a therapeutic context, I use the tools of the Process as a therapist. As we shall see, this therapy is integral to the progress of the individuals in the group from Novices to Initiates. The initiation has nothing to do with any body of belief, but rather with trust, self-awareness and the movement of transformation. The production is going to be a function of the energy and self-interpretation of the individuals and the group. The basic technique of the process is to demonstrate to the participants how the Self expresses its development through symbolic imagery. This is, after all, the source of dream, myth, and all performance. In the early Stages, symbolism is a therapeutic device to be used as such. In this way I function as a therapist.

In the MYTH Stage I become the medium or the coordinator of the mediumistic elements in the group, by which the Myth is evoked. Then I become a director (or the focus of the directorial energy of the group) to stage the Myth. As the later phases of the Process have developed, it has been my preference to have someone in the group specifically take the role of director, and in recent performances I have made an effort to bring an established director into the group who could take over entirely this part of the Process.

In the early days, I used to like to play parts in the production. My definite predilection was to play the Monster, which I did with great flair and relish. I also performed out of the need to test the elements of performing that were being developed. But in time my enthusiasm and need for performing have given way to the necessity of being central coordinator. Playing a role or directing always takes me out of the centered place necessary to bring off the production. During the actual performance, my greatest pleasure is to be simply a spectator.

In the final Stage of the training, the RITUAL, I function as a kind of high priest, very much akin to the role of the head priest in the preparation of ancient ritual-dramas. Basically I focus the iconography of the piece. The group creates the story and characters, but the authenticity of these elements has to be monitored constantly. Every word and action must express the inner truth that the character or action is intended to portray.

A second requirement of this priestly function is to maintain the energy level of the group, a vital element since, in the end, the production is an energy phenomenon. In a way the group has to be able to fly. The energy has to be kept clean of personal detritus and negativity. This cleansing becomes integral to the creative process itself and often feeds the subject matter of the production. Only when the energy is clean can the Ritual reach to the almost superhuman level that is necessary.

The Ritual is an act between gods and man; the high priest monitors this act so that the performers will be able to reach high enough and the gods will descend.

The Basics of Wholeness

The following principles are the basis of the practice in the ORIGINS Process as well as the theoretical base of all my work. I believe that these principles constitute what is genuine in all spiritual and therapeutic work.

The Original YES

In 1970, I was just beginning to recover from a period of low self-esteem. My psyche was just ready to celebrate with a major new insight, a new level of assimilation of the deep truths of Brahmanic mysticism which I had so diligently pursued over two years in India. It was my thirtieth birthday and I was living in a small castle near Lugano, Italy.

There I had the most profound experience of my life. It had nothing to do with outer events, but everything to do with inner lights and realizations. In essence, it was the experience of YES. It was not just *my* YES to existence; it was absolute recognition of *existence itself as a YES.*

This protracted state of *samadhi* lasted about two weeks. Out of it came certain basic knowings. Here they are, boldly stated: The universe is a YES. Self-knowledge is YES. The body is a YES. The heart is a YES. Only the human mind can say NO, and that is a matter of choice. It can also say YES, whereupon it aligns itself once again with the universe.

This absolute YES that I experienced has become the basis of all my work as a thinker, as an artist and as a therapist in practice. It works, too. Behind neurosis there is always some hidden NO. When you find it and say YES instead, the neurosis disappears. This is the basic premise of all the therapeutic and spiritual work in Bodhisattva Arts and ORIGINS.

I believe that every human essence has some kind of genius. Most often it is hidden behind some NO that was first uttered by a parent or a teacher and then buried by many subsequent NOs. These negations become internalized as self-inflicted patterns which infect the mind, inhibit the heart and rigidify the body. Releasing the native genius in each person I work with provides the greatest satisfaction in the work. My highest moments are watching people released for the first time into some wonderfulness they had never before allowed themselves to manifest. It happens a lot in ORIGINS.

In this regard, I always invite the group at the outset to engage in the exercises of the Process as though they were children. "Just play, and draw, and dance, and carry on with the same abandon that you did when you were four, five and six. Consider it all as though you were playing children's games." I had learned from my work with play therapy that this permission has an effect on many levels. It is a validation of the essence, since what we were when we were children is much closer to who we are essentially than is the socialized being that began to develop subsequently. I have also found as a therapist that, short of crisis, the best way to bring people into touch with the realities of their heaviest complexes is to encourage them to enter a child-like state. Participants quickly gravitate to the areas in which there are complexes unresolved from that critical age. And finally there is something for me. I well remember when I was six years old and used to organize the neighborhood kids into making a play. It was magical then, and it is magical now.

The YES is so essential to the ORIGINS Process that we even say YES to the NO. From the beginning it is made clear that the basic issue in the Process is surrender (YES) and resistance (NO). The participants are told that NO has a place too. If anyone wants to say NO to any of the exercises in the process, he has but to stand in the circle and say "I refuse to do this exercise," receive the enthusiastic applause of the group, and be seated to watch the others do the exercise and contemplate his NO. Usually by the time the others have finished, the NO turns to a YES.

Non-performers often come into the workshop with trepidation. But I have rarely seen anyone who cannot perform if he lets himself go. And I am convinced that the greatest performing is a matter of allowing the depths to express themselves authentically. It is a matter of validating the essence more and more deeply.

In the initial, CHAOS Stage, participants are never criticized for their performances. They are encouraged to reach deeper inside, beyond their resistance and self-doubt into a purer and purer source of expression. Each bit of resistance is duly brought forth in the group, and the performers are encouraged to let go into themselves deeper and deeper.

In DREAM and MYTH, participants are told that there is no wrong or right in what they are doing, nor is there any good or bad. These dimensions are waived in favor of the view that whatever they do or come up with is significant, and that significance is what is important. The idea is to say YES to what is coming up, become aware of it and consider its significance in the context of the process.

In the MYTH and RITUAL Stages there is an exercise called Validation in which members of the group tell each other the unqualified positive truth about each other. This exercise of confirming the essence brings the level of the group to almost mystical heights, and performances go on transcending themselves.

For me it is a proven law that people do better—often excelling their highest imaginings—if they are validated for what they are doing well instead of criticized. Even comments on a certain action that a performer may not be doing well are given in the spirit of validating the individual. In moulding the production itself, it is an absolute rule that there is to be no criticism unless there is also proffered a positive suggestion or alternative.

The YES is a fundamental premise of this work. If a member of the group learns the value of this alone, the insight into Self-love that results is well worth the entire experience. The YES produces very practical results. It goes deep into the consciousness of the participants and allows neuroses to be dropped. A positive attitude toward all things is the primary element of authenticity, the catalyst of transformation. And it becomes a basis of confidence by which performances can reach new heights. ORIGINS is all about how to say YES. And YES is the basic utterance of the Divine.

The Establishment of the Witness

The second most important basis of the Process is the establishment of the Witness as the central "character" of each participant and the group process.

What is the Witness?

Consciousness, the most elusive of all concepts and beings, is characterized by awareness. For instance, I am in a room with grey walls and a carpet. I am feeling sadness. Now, I may not realize this or think or it consciously, but at some level there is an awareness of these physical and feeling environments. This awareness element of consciousness is essentially receptive to whatever is given. What is so may or may not be called into active awareness. But if it is, the receptive awareness has already made possible such active awareness.

When this receptive awareness is made active in a purely neutral, non-judgmental and objective way, it simply sees what is so. This "simple seeing" is the *Witness*. The Witness is non-selective, non-judgmental, but active awareness of what is so in consciousness. It does not have values; it simply sees. The mystics call it the eye of God, and it is truly the eye to the Divine because it sees the true YES of existence.

In fact, however, the Witness is seldom experienced as such, because we constantly identify with what is going on and thereby lose the objectivity of the Witness. Moreover, the Witness is always being overwhelmed by the selective judgmental faculties of the mind. Very seldom do we make an observation without some manifest or hidden evaluation. In fact, much

training in mystical schools is to learn how to abstract the objective observation of the Witness from the subtle infringement of the subjective mind.
This discrimination is a basic discipline of any mystical path.

To be in the Witness is to be non-identified with the Self or any of its
aspects. Throughout the Process, participants manifest themselves in many
characters, and it is vitally important that they not be identified with any of
them. In fact, the dramas that are to be presented in the course of the Process
all involve sub-personalities or characters that inhabit the subjectivity of us
all. But this drama is always simply watched by the Witness. In a sense, the
Witness is the prototype of the audience.

At the outset of the training, the participants are asked to make a deep
recognition of this Witness and to commit themselves to its impartial view
throughout the training. A formal covenant is made in the circle as the
members of the group join hands and repeat twelve times slowly and in
unison: "I am the Witness."

The Opening of the Three Centers

Human experience can be divided into three realities. The most
primitive reality is the physical, the sensate, the body. This reality may be said
to radiate from the body center which is located in the middle of the
abdomen, about four finger-widths below the navel. This center is variously
known as the *kath*, the *dan tien*, or the *hara*. It is the literal center of the body
and is the point of origin for all movement in the martial arts. It is also the
internal point of focus for many forms of Oriental meditation.

The second reality is emotion and feeling. This reality may be said to
radiate from the feeling, or heart, center, which is located in the middle of
the chest. This center is the source of feeling, love and intuitive knowing.

The third reality, furthest removed from the primitive sources, is mental:
that reality which can be conceptualized. It radiates from the center of the
head, and is known as the mind center.

The non-awareness of these realities and the blockage and perversion of
their dynamic energies militate against wholeness and health. The standard
profile of a person in the modern West is to be overstressed in the mind
center, and progressively more blocked in the heart and the body centers.
This blockage and the resistance it entails constitute the *ego* and come to be
known in the ORIGINS Process as the Monster.

With regard to these three centers, the purpose of the training is three-fold. The first is to release the dynamic energies of each center: to free the capacity of the body to express itself and to make its reality known; to release the capacity of the heart to feel, to love, and to send forth its wise knowing; to liberate the mind from its stressful control to its greatest possibilities of reflecting what is so with clarity and accuracy. Many dynamic and cathartic techniques are used to accomplish this release.

The second purpose of the training is to clarify these realities and the pure dynamic of each center. Each emits an energy which is perverted in the process of social adaptation. There are few persons who know what a clear impulse of the heart is. Even fewer who know how to interpret the messages of the body. When the three centers and their dynamic realities are clarified, the business and joy of being human become clearer.

The third purpose of the training with regard to these centers is to find the harmony between all three that constitutes authenticity and wholeness. I often describe this harmony with the figure of music. Each center plays its own musical line. The purest music is a melody consisting of a harmony between all three lines. The achievement of this total freedom within each reality, the clarification of the energies of the centers, and the harmonic balance between all three lead to the highest development of the human being. This development constitutes the optimal condition for knowing the Divine. Such a whole, holy person is the ultimate goal of the ORIGINS work.

Thousands of years ago, the geniuses of Asian religious practice discovered that the capacities of these realities of consciousness can be freed and clarified by vibrating the corresponding centers in the body. The vibration was created through chanting, or *mantram*. It is possible to focus the vibration of the voice—according to high or low pitch—in various parts of the body. By focusing the attention on these points of vibration, one can actually affect the corresponding reality. Hence the basic exercise in the ORIGINS training: RAMs in the three centers.

The syllable RAM is the name of the greatest of all Hindu heroes. It is also the name of God. When this name is chanted on a pitch that vibrates in one of the three centers, it has the effect of opening that center.

The RAMs are done as follows. Seven repetitions of the syllable RAM on a very low tone vibrating in the body center; seven repetitions on a medium tone vibrating the heart center; and seven repetitions on a high, nasal pitch vibrating the mind center. The exercise is completed with three repetitions of the low tone to ground the awareness in the body center. This entire sequence is done in complete unison. We call it the "one sound." The image of one sound becomes very significant as the training proceeds.

This exercise provides an ongoing contemplation of several seminal themes: the opening of each center and the clarification of its energies; the harmony of the three centers; the basic paradigm of wholeness in the ORIGINS work, the unity of the group; and, finally, the constitution of the divine human prototype, the one human being of three realities that we all are. In recognition of this one being, we begin and end the RAM sequence with an OM salutation. Each person bows from the waist with his hands pressed together in front of his breast as the group chants on one tone the syllable OM.

This ritual is repeated at the beginning of each work session or the opening of any group meditation. As the ritual opening and harmonizing of the three centers, it represents the end and the essence of the ORIGINS Process.

The Journey through the Process

The Process through which the group passes is extremely intensive and proceeds according to well-ordered steps. The training is an experience of deep self-investigation, expression and creativity in which the performer becomes a pilgrim, a wanderer, a holy man. His purpose is, first, to experience his deepest inspiration as a form of communion with the Divine; second, to come to understand his craft as a form of spiritual discipline; and, third, to experience his art as a path to self-realization and wholeness.

The participants pass through four levels of development. In the CHAOS Stage the participants are called *Novices* and learn to trust their skill in "let-go" performance. In the DREAM the participants, called *Neophytes*, discover the power of the archetypal plot form as the basic formula of the transformation of the Self. In the MYTH the participants as *Initiates* collectively derive a version of the archetypal plot form which expresses its common Self. The group performs this "Myth" improvisationally. In the RITUAL the participants as *Priests* present their Myth as a formal Ritual offering in whatever production form is appropriate.

There follows a detailed and animated description of these four stages.

Stage I: CHAOS

The novices are brought to a point of catharsis where they can give expression, beyond inhibition, to their most primal sources. This basic skill builds the internal confidence of the performer to experience the original Self and to express it before an audience without censorship or design.

The DIONYSIAN: Catharsis and Its Function

The Mothers of Being are the source of all consciousness. They are the dynamic self of the Self, the eternal laws by which we are as we are. They are the basic genetic code of humanity, that by which nature expresses itself as human nature. It is the Mothers of Being that regulate our relation to nature; it is they that punish the sin of *hubris*—human arrogance and pretension. They are absolute, uncompromising, and imminent.

In ancient Greece, Dionysus was the divine form who gave expression to the Mothers. He was followed and worshipped by satyrs, half-man and half-goat, and maenads, wild priestesses who revelled to music that intuited his universality—the energy and power of the Origins.

Socialization, repression and the ideals of civilization do not eliminate these Dionysian elements, for they are the primal stuff of which we are made. Indeed, where these wild impulses are repressed psychologically, they become subversively destructive, causing neurosis, pathology and disease. When they are suppressed culturally, they erupt in violence. Rock and rape, sexual and relational anarchy, lawless paroxysm—these are all forms of Dionysian revenge, gone wild, out of balance. They are the Monster—generated because the Dionysian elements are denied and take revenge. It is the same law psychologically and sociologically.

If the Dionysian elements are freed, if they are clarified and integrated, they serve the totality, originality and higher purposes of man. They are, after all, the Mothers. The cathartic element in primitive theater forms is—as exemplified in Ancient Greece or in Bali—precisely a way of bringing these elements into an integrated state.

The first task of the Novice in the Process is to reach catharsis: to touch the primal Mothers of Being—the dark, raw elements of his own passionate humanity. The ability to enter into the chaos of these primal powers is

48

integral to the transformation process and to the basic communication to be made through the Myth and Ritual. Transformation means that instead of creating Monsters by being at odds with the primal Mothers of Being, we are at one with them—not suffering from their wrath, but integrated with their power. This is the message of the ORIGINS Process as well as its means.

To touch the Mothers of Being is also to release the divine sources of originality. Creativity of any kind is opened up and enhanced by the process of freeing the Self. Hence, there is an ecstasy intrinsic to the expression of our origins that makes the Process alone a blissful end in itself. Whatever the production aims, whatever the goals and purposes of the Process, the mere act of giving expression to the original Self is a form of worship, a way of touching the Divine, an act which is its own reward.

Surrender and Resistance

In this new order where totality becomes more desirable than the ideal, authenticity is valued more highly than morality. For the performer, the realness of being is valued over technique or form.

To be authentic, to be real is to say YES—to surrender to who you really are—in your depths. To be unauthentic is to resist your reality in favor of some inherited or conditioned facsimile of the Self. As you face your essence, so you face God. The reason that performing can be a spiritual discipline is because the skill of the performer in manifesting the truth of his being is the same discipline by which the holy man comes to God. For this reason surrender and resistance are the central issues of the ORIGINS Process. They are the basic content and, finally, the matter to be expressed in dramatic form.

There are many degrees and kinds of surrender. Each has its own corresponding resistance. Since YES is the basis of the training, resistance in its many forms is as important as surrender itself. From the outset the Novices are taught to remain in the Witness with regard to resistance, to keep a constant vigil on it and to allow it to come forth in the many different ways that are provided in the training. Every nuance of resistance is to be brought into individual and group awareness, and often into the dramatization itself.

In the Process, surrender happens in stages. There is first the surrender to the Mothers of Being, to uninhibited expression in performing. The resistance here constitutes all forms of inhibition in the presentation of self.

Second, there is surrender to me as the leader. In the early parts of the training, I tend to exaggerate my natural inclination to appear rather Prussian and Samurai-like, with the result that everyone's neuroses about authority and FATHER get restimulated and brought to the surface. Blocks with authority and resistance to authority figures are major hindrances to surrender at all levels.

Third, there is surrender to the group and its energy. This is symbolized from the beginning as each person is required to surrender to the one sound of the group OM and RAMS. Resistance here is fear of conformity.

Further down the line there is surrender to the production and to the inner truth that each performer must express.

Finally, surrender becomes blissful when, in the performance, the energy of the archetype sweeps the performers up into a mystical communion with the gods. The final surrender in entheotic performance is the "divine reward" of the work and the authentic taste of what it is to be truly surrendered to—indeed, one with—God.

The CHAOS Process

The basic technique of entheotic performing is called simply the Trick. It is basically abandonment, letting fall the restraints on behavior and letting-go to the spontaneous dynamic of the Self beyond predictability or control. The Trick is taught in stages, through techniques that are progressively intended to relax control and sensitize the receptivity to the Mothers of Being as they press for expression from deeper and deeper within.

During each exercise the Novices are asked to remain in the Witness and observe how they surrender and how they resist. Whatever they do is all right; it is simply to be observed, its significance noted. After each exercise, the Novices share in pairs how they were able to surrender and how they resisted. For instance, "I wanted to scream bloody murder, and so I did, but as I was screaming, I suddenly thought, what will they think of me." The pairs then share any important experiences with the group as a whole, and we move on to the next exercise. The effect of the totally permissive ambience and the sharing is to relax resistance. With each exercise, the Novices allow more trust and abandonment.

In the CHAOS Stage, particularly the early portions, the exercises are accompanied by wildly rhythmic music. The Dionysian element, a symbolic intuition of universality, is generated by this music. The ability to move and be moved by rhythm is as important as unbridled expression of feeling and emotion. The response to rhythm is the pulse of the Mothers.

Here are the basic exercises by which the Trick is taught, described in the order in which they occur in the training. Each furthers the capacity for opening and surrender.

Dynamic Breathing and Let-Go
Twelve minutes of rapid, chaotic breathing followed by twelve minutes of total catharsis.

The opening exercise is done to wild, heavily rhythmic music—preferably played by live musicians. The Novices are told to allow themselves total abandonment and to censor nothing that comes up for them. The entire exercise is done blindfolded or with closed eyes.

Here at the outset the Novices are introduced to catharsis, the uninhibited expression of motion. The breathing acts as a kind of affect-bellows. Whatever feelings may be suppressed begin to come up powerfully, their vitality inflated by the chaotic breathing. Normal control can then be abandoned.

The exercise is the first two stages of the Rajneesh Dynamic Meditation. It is called a meditation because it produces a state in which there is no volitional mental activity—a no-mind state. Rajneesh disciples are particularly adept at it. When a room full of disciples or practitioners of primal scream therapy begin to cathart, one hears the mad revenge of Dionysus for twenty centuries of repression. Participants not used to catharsis usually have to do this exercise a number of times before they reach into the deeper levels of abandonment. As the first activity of the training, it functions as a kind of rite of passage, quickly eliminating participants who cannot withstand the rigors of the Process.

What is happening in this catharsis is that the threshold of conscious control is being lowered, and the energy of unconscious affect is being raised so that conscious and unconscious meet. When you become adept at this activity and can remain in the Witness, you experience an awesome detachment in regard to the spectacle of hidden energies exploding from the personal unconscious into consciousness. Already, at the outset of the training, a divine state of wholeness is experienced.

CHAOS: The Novices are brought to a point of catharsis.

Later, you can feel that the unconscious material is no longer personal, but "racial," expressing the unconscious of Western consciousness and of the human race itself.

Isolation Movement

Simple isolated movements of parts of the body are made to rhythmic drumming.

This exercise is repeated several times in the CHAOS Stage. Except for the part that is being moved, the body remains stationary.

The exercise causes the Novice to make movements that are unfamiliar to the body, to break patterns that are ingrained and merely habitual. Thus, the body is prepared to receive and execute movements that are not customary, thereby increasing receptivity to varied expressive possibilities.

The main purpose of this exercise, however, is to develop the sense of difference between making a movement and being moved. There is a distinct kinesthetic difference between a movement that is controlled and one that is abandoned. Novices are asked to observe what it is to control movement and then to abandon the control and allow the rhythm to continue to move them. This builds up a definite physical sense of what it is to surrender, to allow movement to happen as opposed to controlling movement.

Scrambling Activities

Speaking and singing gibberish, nonsense words, words without syntax, then adding dance.

These exercises deal with conscious control; specifically, the inhibitions prohibiting expression that is not rational and ordered in meaning. The purpose is to bring Novices to a place where they no longer feel that their expressions must make some preordained sense.

The exercises constitute a kind of catharsis of meaning. There is much that is human that cannot be expressed in words or syntax; so it remains unknown, unexpressed, unconscious. When you become adept at these dynamic nonsense techniques, the Witness again observes the thrill of deeply unconscious material rushing up into light for the first time—again, a union of the known and the unknown.

All of these exercises are practiced individually and without any audience. The Trick of abandonment has to be mastered internally first. One has to let go of the geometry and rational world of behavior control in favor of a dynamic of being that may have neither geometry nor reason. The validation of these realities constitutes an important teaching in the entire Process: to value that which is anti-social as well as that which is acceptable, the Dionysian as well as the Apollonian. The total being is a dialogue between these two.

Another metaphor that is used to describe the Trick is that of riding a wave, like a surfer. In these scrambling exercises, one waits for an impulse and abandons oneself to it. Just as a surfer finds a wave, rises up on his surfboard and rides with it, so I "step" onto the impulse that is moving me and simply ride it wherever it goes. These aspects of the Trick are mastered before any "performing" is attempted, but they are the rudiments of all further performance in the training.

Ditties
Stand, wait for an impulse, perform a small improvisational piece, wholly spontaneous, without design.

These "ditties" are done first alone, then with an audience of one, then before two others, and then before the entire group. After each sequence, there is feedback with the partners on how surrender and resistance are happening.

These are the culminating exercises in the CHAOS Stage. By the end, each participant can give a short, spontaneous, improvisational performance without preparation or inhibition. It happens very rapidly, and those who at the outset fear performing are in the end quite astonished at how simple it is. One simply rises up on the approaching wave and rides. That is the Trick. It is also the basis of entheotic performing.

Most amazing to me is what I call the "composition factor." You rise up on the wave. It carries you to its climax or breaking and, at a certain point, it stops, and you know to get off. That is to say, the spontaneous Ditty has a beginning, a middle and an end. One does not in any way plan or control it, but there is nevertheless a real composition to the piece. Since the matter of the performance is coming largely from the unconscious, it would seem that the whole Self has a capacity for form and spontaneous organization which is intrinsic and preempts conscious control. The belief is that we have to enforce a conscious form, but the truth is that, if we allow it, a content will

**CHAOS: Participants learn to give expression,
beyond inhibition, to their most primal sources.**

form itself of its own accord. That is to say, composition is intrinsic to the expression of the Self.

As an awareness of this phenomenon dawns on the Novices, they begin to enter into a new trust in themselves beyond control, a trust in the greater Self which has its own built-in controls. This is the true faith in the Dionysian. As trust in this intrinsic control grows, the capacity for surrender increases exponentially. This capacity for trust in the Mothers is the critical aspect of the initiation of the Novice.

Transformation through CHAOS

The "normal" Western neurotic is one who has been uprooted from his grounding in nature, sold out to an unauthentic social view of himself without access to his primal energy and true feeling, and thereby alienated from the great continuum of Self and universe. The CHAOS Stage is an antidote to this condition.

The exercises and process of the CHAOS Stage were originally designed for therapy, for teaching self-expression and trust, and for showing how to achieve the non-volitional state of meditation. The faces of people who have completed these exercises show a remarkable change. There is a brightness, a relaxation, a settling into the being which is apparent to everyone. I myself have experienced the power of these exercises many times and enjoyed the result—that ineffable sense of feeling well within myself, of feeling within myself well.

As I have said, awareness and validation are always authentically thera- peutic. To me they are the basis of all therapy, absolute preconditions for psychological growth. We are partly crazy, irrational, without sense or meaning. The exercises demonstrate that powerfully. All these ways of being are the submerged half of being human. To be able to say YES to this condition is a great relief. It is also healing to become aware of how we resist these aspects out of fear and to realize that much of our resistance is an unnecessary expenditure of vital energy.

Beyond the therapeutic value of awareness and validation, there is the healing that occurs through expression. Self-expression is one of the basic drives of the human psyche. This is the basis of the symbolic function by which every human being expresses his being and process through dreams. This symbolic expression is essential to psychological health. All forms of self-expression are antidotes to suppression, repression, as well as to depression—the three enemies of psychological well-being. Self-expression as a therapeutic mode is the wave of the future, because methods of expression counter the soul-destroying tendency of modern civilization to contain individuality within prescribed forms. This is the basic principle of expressive arts therapies.

Coming to a sense of fulfillment in life has a great deal to do with the capacity for self-expression. Indeed, it may be that the greatest suffering in the world is caused by the fact that so few are able to find means to express the passionate uniqueness in their beings. The Balinese have a beautiful saying: "It is not that every artist is a special kind of person; it is that every person is a special kind of artist." Yet the force of the world is to conform, and all but a handful of people are so oppressed by the circumstances of their lives that they never touch this inner nerve of creative vitality. Every person needs to find the medium through which he can most deeply and satisfyingly express himself. Such a medium provides not only a healing outlet, but also a means for continuing further explorations in awareness through self-expression.

At this therapeutic level, objective aesthetic criteria have no value. The expression is a value in its own right. If one can make a vocation of his art form, so much the better, but far more important is the expression of his own unique being. This is as important as any other single factor in the maintenance of psychological and spiritual health.

The CHAOS techniques have the function of disorganizing the conditioned mask of the individual, because all the behaviors that are called up are either prior to that mask or transcend it. The individual comes first to allow and then to trust that part of himself that does not fall within the parameters of the geometric, the ordered, the rational. The process breaks his identification with these merely acceptable elements and provides a new authentic basis for identity.

The new basis comes as the exercises shake the individual to the roots. The cathartic and dynamic techniques enhance the capacity to feel and experience impulses and emotions of which one has hitherto been only dimly aware.

The rediscovery of primal energy and feeling through unfettered expression provides a new ground for being, a new base of identity that is

more in keeping with who we truly are—this primordial undifferentiated Self
that is one with the entire energy phenomenon of the universe.

Chaos and the Art of Performing

In the ORIGINS training there is a Code of Excellence in performing. Here are
its standards:

- Authenticity of being.
- Visceral quality—the amount of body and heart energy the performance manifests.
- Resonance—the quickening effect of the performance on the audience.

These criteria are all related to the degree and depth of abandonment,
or let-go, that the performer can allow.

The let-go method of performing is characterized first by the capacity
for unfettered cathartic expression. The performer should reach a place
where his physical being can become a pure vehicle for his deepest feelings.
This skill is developed through dynamic exercises as practiced in the CHAOS
Stage.

The second feature of the let-go method is the capacity to ride the wave.
One should be able to catch a wave of being and ride it effortlessly. There
is a distinct feeling of being carried. It is totally effortless and thrilling. There
is no control; only the gentle restraint of inner control. This too is a skill
which is basically spiritual. One has to have great trust to ride these waves.

A third feature of the let-go method is total improvisation. During the
CHAOS Stage, the Novice is taught to use whatever happens, to integrate
spontaneously any happening in the internal or external playing environment, no matter what it is. If the lights go out, use it. If a dog wanders in,
use it. If you slip and fall, integrate it into the performance. If you forget what
is supposed to happen next, use your confusion. Thus the whole internal and
external environment becomes part of the field of the performance. As the
training proceeds, the same rule holds in the Myth and Ritual performances.
The performers always hold the ground.

This policy had its acid test in a performance that we gave once in Los
Angeles. The audience got so caught up in the action that at one point several
of them stormed the stage and started fighting with the performer. I was
tremendously gratified to see that she turned the happening to her advan-

tage, and the attack was integrated beautifully in the performance, so that members of the audience thought it had all been planned. We've had babies wander into the scene, telephones ring, automobiles backfire. When the energy of the performance is high enough, these contributions from the environment become synchronistic, or significantly coincidental enhancements of the action. This too is a feature which requires and inspires trust.

Let-go performing becomes a form of meditation, in the sense that it is an activity not monitored by volitional or controlling behavior. One disappears into a totality of presence. Presence is pure being-energy here and now, responding to what-is, internally and externally, with totality and utter flexibility.

Let-go performing is existentially dangerous. One is always on the edge of the unknown. Even in the performance of the Ritual, when the basic action is set, there is always space left for danger, for improvisation.

Very often, performers who achieve this level of excellence in the ORIGINS training have little or no acting background. In fact, the more polished a performer is in traditional acting technique, or "mask-making," the more difficult it may be to unmask existentially in this way.

In general, it is my experience with actors and performers, both professional and amateur, that the acquisition of mask-making skills is always dangerous, because technique has a way of becoming resistance to authenticity. In some subtle fashion, it fills the gaps of the unknown. An actor who is a real mask maker is not performing dangerously. He is always covered by his technique. Such habits in acting, like all conditioned masks, constitute a resistance to authentic being. They are safe, habitual, but there is no wildness, none of the true blood of life. This bored me so much as a young actor that I felt I had to look elsewhere for the existential danger craved by my spirit.

To me, a consummate performer is one who has totally mastered technique, but can totally abandon it. This is the synthesis of Apollonian form and Dionysian energy. The most gifted performers I have worked with were two Javanese who had both this degree of control and this capacity for abandonment. Their technique was so integrated into their being that they could drop it altogether. That does not mean the technique ceased to exist, but that the pure being resonated *through* the technique. The technique was actually the mode of the pure being. There was nothing conscious or studied about it. The pure being used the technique as style that was totally integrated. It was not there by conscious control. For the most part Western performers are not able to achieve this. They rely existentially upon their acting; their craft amounts to polishing their unauthenticity.

A consummate performer should master technique and improvisation, and he should be equally comfortable in either mode. This range is characteristic of the ORIGINS aesthetic, which always strives for a balance between the most primitive and the most sophisticated, the Dionysian and the Apollonian. Again, I find this combination in its purest expression in the performing arts of Bali and Java.

Entheotic Performance

Entheotic performing is the Trick writ so large as to be cosmic. The god inhabits and expresses itself through the performer. Learning to sustain the disposition of let-go is the core of this kind of performing. A facility for personal catharsis and improvisation are the basic skills prerequisite to the super-personal expression of the gods. These capacities have to be mastered at a personal level until one becomes sufficiently comfortable with the displacement of ego control necessary to channel the expression of elements that are archetypal—super-personal.

As in trance performance, the ego controller is gone. Unlike the trance performer, however, the entheotic performer remains conscious, but consciously withholds his ego-controller. This withholding is the real "craft" of entheotic performance. There is no prelearned content: the content, the substance, is "received" from the Mothers in the moment of performing and delivered forthwith. The performer turns himself over to the Mothers who enter in and use him as their expressive medium.

These skills are the practice for engaging and honoring the Mothers of Being. As the CHAOS Stage draws to a close, the Mothers have touched the Novices so that they have become, in a sense, satyrs—half-human and half-animal. According to Nietzsche, it is out of the chorus of satyrs that Greek Tragedy was born. The satyr heralds an overwhelming sense of unity which leads back into the heart of nature. He is the enthusiastic reveller, filled with transport by the approach of Dionysus. He has touched into the sexual omnipotence of nature. Nietzsche calls this satyr "man's true prototype, an expression of his highest and strongest aspirations."

In adapting these values and the values of the training, one is already on the path of the holy performer. All of the features of let-go performing, together with the skills they require, serve the holy relationship to existence. They all build trust, surrender, authenticity and presence. These are the qualities of an ORIGINS performer and an existential holy man, a whole man. When they are learned, the Novice has entered into an appropriate relationship with the Mothers of Being. He is now ready for his initiation into the secrets of Apollo.

The Initiation into a Religious Language

The transition of the participants from Novices to Neophytes takes place as a function of increasing trust in the expressive power of the greater, non-volitional Self. The insights and experiences that result from the acquisition of the skills in the let-go method of performing result in a new perception of experience in general.

The Novices come to see that existence in an ongoing wave of impulse. At any moment one can surrender or resist. To surrender is to be receptive to the impulse and to realize it through whatever action is appropriate. To choose this impulse and go with it is heroic. As this way of experiencing and choosing existence becomes clarified, the Apollonian begins to arise. A new terminology begins to evolve. As it is a terminology which describes the relationship to existence, it can be seen as the rudiments of a religious language. This language and its terminology of symbols is used throughout the DREAM, the MYTH and the RITUAL.

The wave which the Novice learns to ride is called the "Nature Spirit." It is the impulse of existence, the unfettered movements and emotions "received" from the Mothers. Another aspect of the Nature Spirit is the clarity of internal and external nature that comes with true poise before these waves and impulses.

The capacity to surrender to the impulses, to accede to the primal Mothers, requires the ability to be receptive. In the Love Story, this receptivity is *yin*, or feminine, and we call it the "Heroine." The capacity—equally important—to realize this impulse through action, is essentially active, or *yang*, and we call it the "Hero."

In the Hero's Journey, the active and receptive elements are taken together as the one who chooses to act. This "Heroic Person" may be represented either as a man or a woman. Sometimes I just say "hero." The use of the masculine form is a mere convenience in which no sexism is intended. "Hero" is preferable, that is, easier and more aesthetic than "hero/heroine," just as "he" is preferable to "he/she." The same convenience is used in the language of this book, for which I ask the indulgence and forgiveness of those who are oppressed by the use of masculine pronouns and words to describe what is essentially human.

The inhibiting aspect, the dysfunction of the active/receptive balance and the action of the impulse is called the "Monster." In the sharing that takes place during the CHAOS Stage, this aspect has been clarified in response to the question, "How did you resist?" The Monster is all the judgment, the inhibition, the technique, the mask-making—all that stops the authenticity of Being from expressing itself.

Behind the scene of life and the dramas involving these characters stands the real participant, or "host," who, as the "Witness," observes these symbolic sub-personalities and their interaction, but is identified with none of them.

"Neophyte" means "newly planted." The Novice, now "newly planted" as the Witness in a new experience of trust, a new view of existence, expressed in a new religious terminology, becomes a Neophyte. The Neophytes are like satyrs, now entering into a reality sanctioned by myth and ritual. It is time to emerge out of CHAOS into form, and thus to enter the DREAM.

Summary: CHAOS

The DIONYSIAN: Catharsis and Its Function
    Surrender and Resistance
The CHAOS Process
    Dynamic Breathing and Let-Go
    Isolation Movement
    Scrambling Activities
    Ditties
Transformation through CHAOS
CHAOS and the Art of Performing
Entheotic Performance
The Initiation into a Religious Language

Stage II: Dream

The archetypal plot form (either the Hero's Journey or the Love Story) is introduced. Its psychological significance is discovered and explored. Each participant—now called a Neophyte—experiences and performs himself through his version of each character in the archetype. The Neophyte then acts out his own Dream, his version of the archetypal plot form, playing the several characters. Each psychodramatized Dream is then analyzed by the group. The Neophyte is transformed by the power of the archetype and comes to an understanding of how the Self reveals itself through the archetypal plot form.

The APOLLONIAN: Dream and Its Function

The first Stage of the ORIGINS Process, CHAOS, provides the cathartic opening into the Dionysian aspect of existence and of performance. In the second Stage, the Apollonian aspects are introduced: the elements of divine order, the principle of individuation, and the dream. Apollo is the god of form.

During my undergraduate years, I read voraciously to satisfy my curiosity about dreams and dream theory. It was not until some years later, however, when I was passing through the crisis of synthesizing the East and West within myself, that I had the opportunity to work with my own dreams and thus to come to understand the true magnificence of the dream process and the infinite inner tapestries to which symbol and dream give expression.

One of the most beautiful capacities of the human spirit is the symbolic function. The human psyche has the genius to express itself in images which often have many different levels of meaning. This same expression happens nightly in dreams, through the aeons in myth, and consciously, with craft, through art.

The psyche has this faculty because it has the need for expression. That is why expression is therapeutic. Suppress the symbolic function, and there is psychopathology.

Through dream symbols, experience in general is ordered meaningfully by the psyche. Things are not as they appear in the so-called outer world. The symbols are mysterious ambassadors sent from the deep recesses within to the outer awareness so that the conscious can know the real movements and issues within the unconscious. The symbols emitted by the psyche thus have an integrative function. They are a form of digestion by which new configurations of Self are reorganized out of the old to assimilate the new. They are messages from the mysterious depths that let us know how it is all coming together.

The integrative function, this coming together, may be understood in the context of Jung's thesis on the fundamental drive of the human psyche. The basic process of the psyche is to come together in the wholeness of individuality. The psyche is like a plant. Just as the flowering is programmed into the seed, just so, in the first embryonic cells of the brain, there is the programming for the maturation and flowering of the psyche into wholeness. Jung called this fundamental process and pattern of psychic growth *principium individuationis*, the "principle of individuation." Every human psyche is involved in this process. The primal symbols of dream, taken in their totality, are the ongoing expression which weaves together the fabric of this process of growth.

It is in the context of this evolution into wholeness that "God" is to be understood. Each person's psychological structure includes an independent "religious" function which is the central organizing aspect of the individuation process. Each human being comes with an inborn urge to find a meaning in life. We all have an intuition that we could see ourselves as whole persons, see the ultimate meaning of life, experience ourselves totally.

That wholeness which we seek manifests as a symbol; it surges out of the deep layers of the psyche as what was anciently named the *imago dei*, the "god-image." The god-image flows out of the psyche, manifesting our deep-rooted urge toward wholeness and unity. This spontaneously rising image, the imprint of what we seek, is the root source of our intuition that there must be something higher than this "I" that pulls together all of life and all of phenomena, and that reveals to us the meaning of life. It creates in us a sense that the unitive vision—indeed, the unitive principle or spirit—is possible. Thus our need to explore the far reaches of our unconscious and our need for a religious life are one and the same.

Since dream is the symbolic medium of the relationship between the mysterious inner sources and the outer world of conscious realities, psychological and spiritual health have to do with the expression of the symbols and the intuitive understanding of their integrative messages. Conversely, pathology is a result of being alienated from these symbols and their meaning. This is why the interpretation of dreams is the core of psychoanalysis. It restores a sense of integration by bringing about Self-awareness through the interpretation of the symbols produced by the psyche.

In *Modern Man in Search of a Soul*, Jung explains that the pathology of modern man is caused by the particular character of his alienation from his inner world: Since he has sold himself out to rational and objective consciousness, he cannot allow for what is mysterious and rationally unaccountable; if experience cannot be programmed into the computer of the rational mind, it does not exist. This is why the scrambling exercises in the CHAOS Stage were so important—to give place to what is not subject to rational expression or understanding.

There is also in modern man a prejudice to see the world projected by the so-called objective sciences as the only viable reality. Hence, the symbolism in dream and myth, which is so integral to the health of the soul, gets disregarded as having no real meaning or value. This disregard for the ambassadors of the gods places man in the greatest peril. These are the Origins that the ORIGINS Process is intended to reinstate.

The Archetypal Plot Forms

Since my intellect first awakened and engaged with the real quest of my life, I have been fascinated with what is most ancient in me. Even as a child I had a sense that something of my roots had been lost before I was ever born. I knew that whatever my quest might be, for whatever future boon of knowledge, it would not be truly new unless it included the most ancient. These two words, "primal" and "primordial"—which held such a fascination over me—carried with them an aura of lost, but vital meaning. They evoke what is earliest, yet still present, and absolutely basic. Whatever these Origins were, I knew that they must be universal, that they must belong to every human being and, as I subsequently understood it, to the ONE human being that we all are.

Archetypes

In my quest for the most ancient, I came upon Freud's formulations of personality: the ego, superego and id. These were fascinating, but they somehow denied the poetry of the human spirit. They were in fact scientific conceptions. More appropriate, somehow, were the terms used in the formulations of Jung: persona, shadow, anima and animus. But somehow the same feeling of frustration was there; they too were scientific conceptions. Somewhere in his conception of archetypes, however, Jung definitely had the key.

The symbolic function of the psyche produces its own images of itself and its parts, and they are not conceptual or scientific terms. I never felt quite right about describing the essence of mankind in concepts. But through symbols I could begin to recognize the human spirit in a way that seemed to fit the case.

An archetype is a primal form in which experience arranges and expresses itself symbolically. Archetypes represent the basic quantities, qualities and entities of the universal human psyche. They are meaning forms that are common to all human beings through time.

An archetype has two aspects: the symbolic form and the elemental aspect or experience of the psyche that the image expresses. The symbol and its double. Thus a beautiful woman may represent the intuitive, feeling, receptive aspects of being. A handsome man may represent the rational, active aspects of being. A womb represents the source of the psyche. A circle represents the completion of the individuation process. The image of God represents the possibility of wholeness. And so on. It is because there are archetypes that we can speak of the collective psyche of humanity. This repository of all archetypes Jung called the "collective unconscious." Contemplating the archetypes within, through dream and myth, allows us to contemplate and comprehend the prime movers, the gods without.

Joseph Campbell explored Jung's formulations in the field of anthropology, studying the actual appearance of archetypes in the myths and dreams of many cultures all over the world. Here for the first time was a real study in the world-field that was to produce truly universal forms.

The Plot Forms

Every time we turn on the television, see a movie, watch a play or read a novel, we see the same stories over and over again. The same basic plots are moving before us. The particulars are always changing—the settings, the circumstances, the qualities of the characters, the issues surrounding the plot—yet the basic stories are the same. In time, I have come to see that the psyche has a *fundamental need* to relate to these patterns. This "need" is the reason that we value the story arts. The fact is that *the primal plot forms tell us, on many subliminal levels, how to go about our own process of individuation.* Our psyche needs them as guides, as maps. Conversely, the archetypal plot forms express the basic laws of the individuation process.

These archetypal plot forms are "primal" in two senses. First, every plot is reducible to them. They are the basic logic of story. You cannot find a story, ancient or modern, a dream, a legend, a myth, that does not in some way manifest these forms or some fragment thereof. Second, they are the expression of the fundamental growth or movement of the human psyche. They express the laws of the process of individuation. The work of ORIGINS is always a penetration into the inner significance of these forms and an expression of their power to bring about transformation.

In his book *The Hero with a Thousand Faces*, Joseph Campbell reduces all myths to one formulation, the Hero's Journey. Such a reduction is possible, but for reasons that will become clear, I have reduced them to *two* archetypal plot forms: the Hero's Journey and the Love Story. Briefly, they are as follows:

The Hero's Journey is the archetypal plot form that expresses the nature of all psychological change, from the simplest acquisition of a new insight through all the difficult changes life brings, to enlightenment, to psychotic breaks. The action of the archetype moves in a circle:

Separation—the Heroic person at home, the call to adventure, the meeting with the Magic Helper, the gift of the Magic Implement.

Initiation—the battle with the Monster at the threshold, the crossing of the threshold into the land of adventure, and the Supreme Ordeal.

Return—the reward, the flight and the return home, creating a new status quo.

The Love Story is the archetype of the union of opposites as represented by the lovers—hero and heroine. I sometimes call it the "androgyne archetype" because its inner meaning is the alchemical figure of the union of the masculine and feminine elements of the psyche. The action is as follows:

The lovers are together in primordial unity; the Monster distracts the Hero and abducts the heroine; the Nature spirit appears and makes one or both lovers aware of what has happened and presents a Magic Implement with special powers; the Hero overcomes the Monster with the help of the Magic Implement; the Hero and Heroine are reunited.

These two universal plot forms are the essence of dream, myth, the principle of individuation, the basic forms by which the human psyche organizes itself and moves through the manifold levels of transformation. They are the realm of Apollo.

There are two ORIGINS trainings. Each is based on *one* of the two forms only, but the plot forms are used in the same way in both trainings. For instance, in the Love Story training, the Love Story archetype is introduced at the outset of the training. The language and terminology of the CHAOS Stage is based on its four characters—the hero, the heroine, the Monster and the Nature Spirit. In the DREAM Stage the archetype of the Love Story forms the basis for the Dream of each participant. In the MYTH Stage, the Myth that the group collectively creates is based on the Love Story archetype, and this same Love Story forms the basis of the Ritual production.

Therefore, to experience both archetypes—which I recommend to all participants and *require* for all performers who take part in major ORIGINS productions—two trainings are necessary: The Hero's Journey and The Love Story. Oddly, it does not seem to matter which of the trainings is done first. There are subtle advantages and disadvantages to doing them in either order.

The DREAM Process

In the DREAM Stage, the Neophytes, fresh out of CHAOS, are "newly planted" in a basic view of existence and a language by which they can describe their experience of this new view. The figures in this new religious language correspond with the characters in the archetypal plot form which is introduced at the outset of the DREAM and is the basic form from which the plot of the Myth is derived and the production is created for the Ritual.

The DREAM Stage lasts from three to seven days. During this time the Neophytes experience in depth the characters within and the action of the archetype, often undergoing in the process a deep transformation.

The first experience of creating my own Hero's Journey was in 1973 when I co-led a Hero's Journey Workshop at Esalen with my friend Paul Rebillot. Paul had put together an ingenious series of Gestalt exercises into a basic process whereby the participant created and acted out his own version of the characters and action of the Hero's Journey. It was a tremendous thrill for me, because, although I had studied the archetype for years, I was now able to create the image of my own hero and participate in his journey. It was rather like experiencing the analysis of one's own dreams for the first time after studying dream theory for years.

In the DREAM Stage of the ORIGINS Hero's Journey, the basic Gestalt process developed by Paul is used, with some alterations and additions based on my own sources, particularly my work in India and in the Arica Institute. I created the Love Story training out of further modification and adaptation of this brilliant series of exercises.

To give an idea of what it is like to pass through the DREAM Stage, here is a description of the Hero's Journey Process which each participant in the DREAM experiences as he creates and dramatizes his own Hero's Journey:

After the archetype is presented to the group, the Neophytes set out on their own journey. Each begins with a comprehensive survey of the home or their present *status quo*. Then each creates and explores his Heroic Person, his Magical Helper and the Implement of power, and his Monster who guards the gate to the Land of Adventure.

Each Neophyte stages and performs before the group his own version of the first part of the journey in which the Hero leaves home and meets the Magic Helper who presents the Magic Implement and clarifies the magic power which the Hero then uses to overcome the Monster. The group gives feedback on each performance, and I do a brief analysis of each Dream.

Having thus overwhelmed the Monster, the Neophytes pass through the Threshold of Adventure and are led into the Supreme Ordeal where each confronts his most elemental fear, that which underlies the power of the Monster. The psychodramas of each ordeal are supplemented with deep analyses and Gestalt work so that the energy suppressed under the fear and revealed by the Ordeal can be freed. Finally, each receives the boon of new strength and knowledge and is brought home, newly transformed, able to move through life in a new way.

By coming to see their own being and transformation through the magic lens of the archetype, the Neophytes are initiated into the mysteries of the plot form and its powers, an initiation necessary to participation in the MYTH and RITUAL Stages.

The DREAM Stage consists primarily of two parts: the creation and analysis of the characters and the psychodrama of the Neophyte's Dream and his version of the archetype.

The Evocation and Analysis of the Characters

The evocation and exploration of the characters, or archetypal subpersonalities, constitutes about half of the DREAM Stage. It takes three to five hours for each character. Each is evoked out of an experience of the principle represented by the character, by embodiment of the attributes and by penetration into subconscious imagery. The character that is evoked is important in itself, but equally significant is the Neophyte's reaction to his characters.

The characters constellate the archetypal aspects of the psyche. I have often been told by participants in the trainings that it is far more helpful to speak of these different aspects as characters, rather than to use scientific or conceptual terms. It is more personal, more quickening to speak of "my heroine," or "Demeter," than to speak of "my anima" or "my *yin* side" or "my inner woman." There is also an element of humor which is valuable, especially when dealing with the character of the Monster. This humor, always a catalyst, is actually part of the transformation itself. To speak of "Mud" rather than "my self-destructive tendencies" or "my negativity" also propels the matter into the realm of fairy tale. This mythologizing is healing in its own way and tends to enhance awareness rather than to distract from it. Somehow when you have a conceptual handle on an insight, it degenerates from true self-awareness to mere knowledge, which, alas, has little transformational value.

An example of the creation of a character is the evocation of the Heroic Person in the Hero's Journey. The Neophytes are asked to move about expressing certain types of heroes—a mythological hero or heroine, a movie hero, the first heroic person from childhood, etc. They are asked to write ten characteristics of the heroes they have portrayed. They then dance a hero's dance, shouting out each characteristic one by one as they embody it energetically in their movement. They are then brought into deep relaxation and taken through a guided fantasy in which they meet and converse with the inner Hero evoked by their dance. They memorize this fantasy, draw a flag or crest representing the various aspects of their Heroic person, and make a dramatic presentation of themselves as the Heroic Person before the group. All of this takes at least three hours.

The purpose of these exercises is to evoke the characters or sub-personalities out of the unconscious and to bring the Neophytes into awareness of the characters as aspects of himself. Some of the methods for doing so are as follows:

Movement and Stance

The body is the seat of the unconscious. This is a basic tenet of many modern therapies and is particularly well developed in Gestalt therapy and in Arica. The unconscious expresses itself through the body; this we call body language. This language can be read as a primary source for the characters.

It is also possible to instruct the consciousness by placing the body in an appropriate static position that expresses a certain mood or character. I call this a "stance." It is an adaptation of the Indian practice of *mudra* contemplation, which was an important part of the Arica work. A mudra is a position of the body, usually involving some positioning of the hands. For instance, in the mudra of detachment, one is seated, cross-legged and perfectly straight, the backs of the hands resting on the knees with palms open. One sits for long stretches of time in that position contemplating internally the kinesthesis, the inner sense of one's body. The repose instructs one's concentrated awareness, clarifying the kinesthetic intuition of the attitude, the inner essence of detachment. In a similar way, a performer "sculpts" his own body into expressive forms that can be "read" by others. In the ORIGINS training these two ways of using stances are combined.

Each character that is created has a characteristic stance which each Neophyte must discover for himself. To contemplate the true inner being of the character, they are asked to remain in this stance for a long time. Before they perform a character, they are told to take the appropriate stance and breathe deeply until the character begins to live from within.

There are movement forms that work in the same way. For instance, in creating the Hero in the Love Story, the group does Karate movement to discover a pure *yang* attitude and as a method for clearing (and seeing resistance to) pure *yang* spaces.

There are also meditations on the form of the body itself. When the group is creating the Heroine, for instance, they experience the woman's body as the embodiment of the *yin* principle. They are asked to lie on their backs. Slowly I instruct them to envision each part of their body as a woman's body. For the women, it is an awareness exercise; for the men it is a projection exercise, to allow them to experience the feeling of having a woman's body.

Of course there is also movement to express and to evoke each character. For instance, in the creation of the Heroine, the Neophytes are asked to rise and dance after the body visualization as though they were the woman they projected, dancing for her lover. This contemplation occurs just before the Neophytes enter the guided fantasy where they first meet their Heroine. These movement aspects prepare the psyche by focusing upon the bodily character of the expressive movement.

Perhaps the most powerful experience in the training is the evocation of the Monster out of the body. Neophytes are put in touch with the chronic tensions in their bodies. Then, through a cathartic process accompanied by cymbals and drums, they exaggerate these tensions until their bodies become totally distorted by them. Cries giving expression to the pain of these tensions are evoked, and the monstrous manifestations of these total tensions do a wild Monster dance. This is the most cathartic exercise in the Process. If the Neophyte can get into it totally and *become* the Monster, it can also be a moment of transformation.

Guided Fantasy

Guided fantasy is a device for evoking the imagery of the unconscious. The participants are put into a near-hypnotic relaxation and taken through a spoken fantasy in which their own imagery fills out the forms that are spoken. Each of the characters is discovered through such a guided fantasy.

It is critical that the participants trust whatever comes to them during the guided fantasy. Often people will change the images if they don't like what is coming up, a very insidious form of resistance. The unconscious is always right, though it is not always possible for the conscious mind to accept or understand immediately what it brings forth. This trust is all part of learning to trust the Mothers of Being.

Dream: The inner characters are discovered through guided fantasy.

The Nature Spirit is evoked for each Neophyte by some item that is found in nature and brought into the tribal circle of the group. The Neophytes are taken into a ritualized guided fantasy in which they experience the Spirit who "gave" them the item, clarifying its magical, but very pertinent, power. A rose becomes the power to transform each situation with love; a stone becomes the power to still the mind with eternal wisdom; a twig becomes the power to see growth in all things.

Art Expression

In several cases the participants are asked to draw either the characters themselves or some symbolic form of the character. For instance, when the Monster Dance is stopped abruptly, the Neophytes are suddenly asked to envision the appearance of the Monster they were expressing in their dance. These drawings are used in the presentations and the subsequent analysis of the characters.

Presentation Performances

The work on each character culminates with a presentation in which each Neophyte presents himself before the group as the character he has created. The content generated by the guided fantasy is used as a base upon which to improvise the presentation.

The Monsters are enacted in a particularly important part of the Process in which each must submit to questioning by the group. These questions are intended to increase the awareness of the Neophyte about his Monster and how it works, an awareness that is vital to the transformation process as well as the general understanding of the nature of the Monster.

Through these techniques and others, each character in the archetype is evoked, analyzed and personified in a performance. Each character is an unconscious dream element that is made manifest and brought into awareness. The psyche of each Neophyte has now created its own unique symbolic language.

In the following section we will have the opportunity to see examples of two Dreams. Taken together, the characters in each of the archetypal plot forms constellate a complete individual psyche. It is possible to create a psychological profile of the host Neophyte through the analysis of the characters and their interaction in the story line of the archetype, making possible a basic

Dream: Each Neophyte discovers and portrays his Monster.

analysis of the psyche of each Neophyte. We call it a "mini-analysis."

In the training, this analysis of the characters gives the Neophytes insight into their own process, but also teaches them, as part of their initiation, how to understand dream (myth) characters and their meaning and value in expressing the Self. In this way, the Neophytes are being trained to become creators and interpreters of dream and myth.

The Action and Analysis of the Plot Forms

The second aspect of the plot forms is the action in which the characters interact, exchange energy and alter each other. This constitutes the dynamic of the archetype, its force and the internal movement of the transformation process.

Once the characters have been created, performed and analyzed, the story line of the archetype is presented and each Neophyte is asked to create a story using the characters that have been evoked and the outline of the action of the plot form. This "Dream" is then presented to the group in a small archetypal psychodrama with the Neophyte playing all the characters himself.

Again, it is important that the story come as much as possible from the unconscious. A good device for reaching the unconscious is to catch the group off guard. Sometimes I tell them that they must create the story and an improvisational psychodrama with fifteen minutes preparation. At other times I give them overnight to write a story, and then next morning I tell them suddenly that they are to dramatize this story in a small improvisation. It varies with each group, but in general a long preparation does not necessarily facilitate matters, not does it provide stories that are less consciously contrived. Each way has its own advantages.

In any case, creating a story is not terribly difficult to do because as soon as the characters are created and filled out in their various distortions and dilemmas, the action is almost implicit and only a matter of filling in a few blanks.

The dramatization of each Neophyte's story is the culmination of the DREAM. Each participant has to do everything for his own production. He writes the story (though the performances are always improvised in the end). He must play all of the characters (sometimes there is a narrator, or the Neophyte includes the Witness as one of the characters). He directs, stages and costumes. Since one person is playing all three or four characters, the costume changes have to be quite fast and preferably quite clever.

These mini-performances are the highlight of the Dream Process. Almost everything I loved about creating theater as a child, and almost everything that is present in these productions was lacking for me in my early experiences with traditional theater. They are not just drama, but the drama behind all drama. It is true theater of the Self.

Sometimes the performances are done in pantomime, sometimes in dance, sometimes in gibberish. By this time the Neophytes are quite secure that they are not being judged. I have also never for a moment let on that there may be any reason to consider such performing difficult. Because of the CHAOS training and this attitude, the Neophytes are relieved of this Monstrous pressure, and they simply fly, almost always far exceeding any idea they might have had of what they are capable of doing. It is wonderful, and a good time is had by all—especially me.

In the feedback and analysis sessions that follow the psychodrama performances, each Neophyte receives vital and extensive information about who he is and how his essential life-drama is working itself out. The feedback sessions are sometimes enhanced by showing video recordings of the performances. Feedback is twice as potent if the performer has had the benefit of seeing himself and is thus able to contribute to the discussion as another observer.

Each Neophyte begins his analysis session by telling a summary of the story he portrayed. The group gives feedback. The person describes how the story expresses his own inner drama, and this is followed by comments from myself and the group. The person then tells what he allowed himself that he had never allowed before. Finally, the group discusses the excellence of the performance. If there is some issue in the psychodrama that was not resolved, we will perform it as a group, bringing the unresolved conflict into some resolution. Sometimes, if there is time, I also do individual analytic sessions with each person.

The DREAM Stage, together with its feedback, constitutes a mini-psychoanalysis. If the participant has entered deeply into his process and allowed himself a real catharsis on any of the many levels that are possible through the Process, he experiences a significant expansion of personal awareness and power. Drastic changes often take place. Thus, each Neophyte is brought to a deep understanding of the process of transformation and its tangible manifestations.

Integral to the initiation of the Neophyte is the understanding of how the Self expresses and reveals itself through the symbolism of the archetype and how the archetype portrays the dynamic process of real transformation. This is grasped only through intuitive understanding gained by experience with the archetype and the Dreams produced by the group. It is the actual understanding of these mysteries that constitutes the initiation of the Neophytes. At this stage they are coming to this understanding, first by experiencing the process and symbolism as it reveals each his own Self, and second by seeing how it works in the case of the other participants.

Through the understanding of dream symbolism and its power to express the Self, the Neophytes become initiated into the mystery of the archetypes and adept at translating the experience of one's own subjectivity into symbolic forms. This ability on the part of each Neophyte is essential to the next stage of the Process—the creation of the Myth.

Two Dreams and Their Analyses

Now that we have seen how the DREAM Process is carried out, we can turn to the real content of the experience. There follows an expanded description of each archetypal plot form followed by a Dream corresponding to each, together with the analysis of the Dream. The first of these Dreams is from a participant in a Hero's Journey training and the other is from a participant in a Love Story training.

The word "transformation" is often used lightly in "New Age" circles. In the ORIGINS Process, its meaning is very specific. Before discussing transformation in abstract terms, the detailed analysis of the archetype, the characters, and the action of the story will provide concrete and detailed clarification of the existential reality of transformation in the context of these actual case histories.

These Dreams and their histories typically express the individual process and transformation of the participants who created them. I have chosen these two in particular because they afford a vivid constellation of metaphors for the issues in this book and the cultural pathology with which ORIGINS is concerned. Individuals are holograms of their culture. Dreams that express a culture and a time are, in their own right, myths. These two Dreams are, in my opinion, evocative myths of our time.

A Hero's Journey: The Archetype of Change

This archetypal plot form expresses the nature of any psychological change, from the simplest acquisition of a new insight, through all the difficult changes life brings, to major psychotic breaks, to enlightenment.

The Hero's Journey has three characters—the Heroic Person, the Magic Helper and the Monster—and a fourth character element which appears in the Supreme Ordeal. The action of the archetype moves in a circle: The Heroic Person is home, receives a call to adventure, meets with the Magic Helper and receives a Magic Implement, which is used to battle with the Monster at the threshold. Triumphant, the Heroic Person crosses the threshold, confronts the Supreme Ordeal, receives a reward and returns home.

The inner movement of the archetype is separation from the status quo, initiation and return. As the archetype of all change and transformation, the Hero's Journey is also the basic form of all initiatory rites, from time immemorial.

Charlotte's Dream

Charlotte was a beautiful and intelligent Southern lady, in her mid-forties, who was an executive in a large business machine corporation. She was struggling to overcome a lifetime of inhibitions imposed by the rigid religious training she had received as a Christian Scientist child in a fundamentalist Southern community. She felt this background had robbed her of her chance to fulfill herself as a woman.

The following is Charlotte's two-part Dream. It was created and enacted in the workshop and subsequently written by her into this form.

> One brilliantly sunny morning, Isaiah, the ascetic, was sitting in his only chair on the main floor of his spartan house. After meditating a few minutes, he sent his flag up the pole outside his house.
>
> The air was clear and pure. The light on the meadow made it suddenly luminous, instead of dry and barren as usual. His eyes rose to the horizon, where he saw in the far distance a tiny figure. He strained and squinted to see what it could be. The figure was gamboling and

playing, but its nature was indistinguishable. Visitors and wildlife were rare on his hill, so he resolved to see what this vision could be. He took a walking stick and began to cross the yellow meadow by the path heading toward the rollicking black figure.

Isaiah strode briskly, invigorated by the air, stimulated by curiosity. Halfway toward the figure, he lost sight of it for a moment. Then it rose suddenly from the grass, and he saw its outline more clearly. It was a girl, which caused a feeling of inner recoil in Isaiah. He didn't want to see a girl. But then as he strode closer, he saw it was just a girlish figure with frills and ribbons on its costume of every shade of green. In fact, there may have been twenty or thirty hues of green in the fantastic garb of this creature who sparkled as he moved with many sensuous fabrics in all shades of blue and green. It was Puck.

As Isaiah arrived at the clearing where the being continued to dance, he saw to his amazement that he was dancing around a pool of water fed by a bubbling source. The colors of his costume were mirrored in the water. (Or was the shimmering water mirrored by the creature?) The pool was surrounded by flowers—white pond lilies, water iris, silver water weeds, water Hawthorne. And before Isaiah could interrogate this dancer, the sprite seized him by the arm, and the two of them plunged into the water—down, down, not into the dark, but into water radiated with light.

While swimming underwater, Isaiah felt at home; he was a fish, a water sprite. While they were swimming, his companion thrust one of the white flowers into Isaiah's hand, put a finger to his lips, smiled and swam back to the surface.

Isaiah swam on. He saw a round cave, bright with light. This attracted him, so he swam toward it.

But as he approached, tentacles came out from the rocks on either side of the round opening, and he became entangled in them. It was the Monster, Mud. The more he struggled against the tentacles, the more he was enlaced and wrapped up by their narrow, undulating movements. He began to fear strangulation or drowning. Could he remain in the water forever? Would his life be snuffed out here? Was this the end?

As he began to lose hope, his eye caught the white lily, still clutched in his hand without his being aware of it. Why did he have it? It must have a significance. But what? He managed, in spite of the web of weeds binding him, to bring the flower to his nose to smell it. Then he immediately thought: "This is ridiculous. I can't smell underwater!" But, miraculously, he could.

An overwhelming, evocative odor of all he had loved—jasmine, rose, gardenia, honeysuckle, carnation, and the smell of mown grass after rain, the essence of the sweetness of centuries crushed into one inhalation—blew the water and the tentacles away.

He awoke in the meadow, but it was green, not yellow. It teemed with insects; it was covered with Marguerites, poppies and blue wildflowers. Dragonflies and butterflies vied for the nectar of its flowers. Birds sang, and a kingfisher dived into the pool that now had grown still.

* * *

In the midst of the meadow, now green, I saw an arched oaken door made of massive, dark planks. I opened it to see an earthen tunnel from which a warm light was coming. After taking the path up the tunnel, I came across a horrible sight.

It was a huge, ugly, diseased blob of indeterminate shape, different colors and foul corruption. It was a huge sore with no shape. All was disintegration, decay and rot. There was no head. I was horrified and didn't want to touch it. I wanted to jump over it.

Puck appeared and took me by the waist. He said we had to walk through it. It made my ankles sting and it clung to me.

Puck told me I had to keep walking, and then he pushed me through a small hole into a bright, fiery space which evaporated, vaporizing the blob. It was safe in this bright, warm space. It didn't burn me. I remained and rested.

From the light, warm space, I went through a blue curtain into a room with an altar on which stood my reward—a gold crescent moon.

A wise old man stood next to the altar. He told me that the crescent moon was called "Violet." I asked him what it should do for me. He said it would make me whole. "How?" "By showing it to people—not literally, but by showing your moon qualities." Then I asked, "What? How do you mean?" He said: "By looking at everything as if it were in your inner warm space. By relating to the external world as linked to that warm space, and treating it, seeing it differently."

Then the old man told me to take the crescent moon up to the top of a mountain and put it there with the sun shining on it. It became blindingly brilliant, like a star. Then I brought it down into the room, here and now.

The Characters

In the archetypal plot form of the Hero's Journey, the Heroic Person may be figured either as a man or a woman or as any sort of animal or creature. I usually refer to it simply as the Hero. It represents the aspect of the Self that is volitional and inclined to move forward. It is that part of us that steers and presses on, no matter what the obstacles.

Charlotte's hero, Isaiah, was unusually negative, almost an anti-hero. This showed immediately the bankruptcy of the life projected by Charlotte's ideals, a circumstance central to her entire journey. Isaiah was a wizened old man with a white beard, moustache, and no hair on his head. He was a kind of depressed God-image, a collapsed metaphor representing the "god that has fled." He wore a white robe and lived in a grey house with an arched doorway on a hilly meadow covered with yellowish grass. His favorite room was like a prison or monk's cell, a basement with brick walls and a brick floor. Presumably the drain and the drainpipe in the corner were there to keep him from any contact with water—the giver of vitality. There was an iron ring and one tiny window in the brick wall, and the room was furnished with one wooden chair. Sparse, indeed.

This hero represents Biblical morality carried to its ascetic anti-life extreme. Named after the doom-saying Old Testament prophet, Isaiah was devoid of any vitality or love. This was underlined by his wizened countenance and aquaphobic nature. He well symbolizes the extremely ascetic and bloodless worldview created by Charlotte's austere self-discipline and the rigid misinterpretation of Christian Science ideals with which she had been raised and which she had long since adopted as her own. This background of ideals was compounded by her own extraordinary discipline of mind, a heroic characteristic that led her up the ladder of success in the highly competitive male world of corporate business.

In a way Isaiah represents the superego hero tempered by years of reaction to Mud, the morass of guilt. He wanted to outstrip Mud with his ascetic discipline and imposed purity. It is unusual for the participant (the host) to be so ambivalent toward the Hero. Charlotte was very angry about Isaiah, feeling that it was he who had prevented her from living out her nature as a woman. The ambivalence toward her own ideals was a source of great pain in Charlotte's life. But the mission of Isaiah was to be wise, and in the guided fantasy in which he appeared, he told Charlotte that what he most needed from her was her heart.

The Monster is in many ways the possibility for a true engagement with the Origins. In the Hero's Journey, the Monster manifests in three ways, each deeper and closer to the core.

The first manifestation is expressed in the resistance of the Hero to leave the home, the "refusal of the call to adventure." In Charlotte's story, Isaiah doesn't want to go any further when he thinks the attractive figure gamboling in the sunshine is a girl. He recoils, wanting to return home. Behind this conservative attachment to the status quo is a fear of the unknown. Already the Monster is present, but not apparent: "Better to stay at home where things are safe and no one can get hurt." Or, "If you think things are bad now, wait'll you get out there where nothing is sure."

The second manifestation of the Monster in the Hero's Journey is the guardian of the gate who prevents the Hero from entering into the Land of Adventure. Here the Monster is clearly the fearful inhibitor of the Hero, stopping him from entering further into the mystery to which he is attracted. The Monster is saying NO to the essence. This is the clue, vital to the understanding of transformation, that the Monster is created out of the negation of essential energy.

As the inhibitor in the archetype of change, the Monster stops us, says NO to what is essential. It manifests as fixed and rigid beliefs in the mind; it stops feeling, emotion, love and the intuitive messages from the heart; and it holds tensions and patterns of tension in the body. It usually plays on some chronic physical weaknesses and always overcomes the heroic impulses in certain habitual situations. I often say that the Monster's first characteristic is that it hides. This is because it constantly throws out a smoke screen of blame and because its greatest enemy is awareness. The most insidious Monsters are always found in those who start by denying that they have one at all.

In Charlotte's case, it is hardly a wonder that her Monster is Mud, since she is a woman of such studied immaculateness. Mud is like a spider, who binds Charlotte with his web and does not allow her to move, suffocating her. Charlotte's rage at this Monster is very great. She felt that this guilt and fear (in league with Isaiah) had robbed her of her ability to enjoy life, sensuality and sexuality. Meanwhile, Mud attacks Charlotte's back, often giving her lots of pain and discomfort. She is slightly stooped from him. His basic message to her is that she is too sensual and thus morally wrong, that in reality she is unattractive, and that her real self is not lovable. Ironically and touchingly, when Charlotte portrayed Mud she appeared in a black mink coat.

The third manifestation of the Monster in the Hero's Journey takes place in the Land of Adventure. The Supreme Ordeal is the initiation, the heroic confrontation with the symbolic representation of that in the Self which is most feared. For Charlotte, this character element was a mass of shapeless disease.

Usually this character element obscures some basic power of the Mothers that is hidden behind tremendous fear. In this sense it is the generating source of the Monster, the nexus of the complex. Hence the existential meaning of the Monster. At the base is the Mothers of Being, an aspect of which—sex energy, anger, nothingness or death (in Charlotte's case, organic mess)—is unacceptable and elicits deep fear. This fear and the element it negates create the Monster, a complex of self-negation that is continually fed by the ongoing rejection of the Mothers through fear.

Against this complex is pitted the Hero, the conscious, volitional self, which is aided by the synchronistic powers of the Magic Helper sent forth by the Mothers of Being who would bring the entire Self back to oneness. The Magic Helper comes forth to give synchronistic help when we have heroic courage to step out from our status quo. We were stuck and nothing happened. But if we take a step, some help comes forth. It may be some new awareness; some new power or faculty that we did not know we had; or a person who can give us new information. It always happens, and the power that is bestowed always turns out to fit the tests that are to come. This is part of the magical power of the archetype that has to be experienced and brought to attention in order to be believed.

In Charlotte's story, the Helper was the trickster Puck and the implement was the "Magic Key," the white lily with the power of soul.

Puck is colored every kind of green, all the shades of regenerate nature. This trickster's name barely misses being "fuck." He is the antidote to Isaiah—joyous, elusive, quick, clever and lively. These elements characterize another part of Charlotte's nature, the part that had been set aside for most of her way up the ladder of moral excellence and worldly success. It is this playful ambassador of the Mothers who inspires Isaiah to initiate his quest to regain the wisdom of the heart.

The Magic Key bestowed upon Isaiah was a white lily that had been found in the mud (in the negated fun?). It had the timeless power of Soul, "the essence of the sweetness of centuries." With this implement growing out of the mud ("fuck" cultivated into "Puck," vitality cultivated into beauty), Isaiah was able to escape from the clutches of Mud. The power of the Magic Implement was to return Charlotte to what she essentially is, to allow her to be open, to savor the perfumes of the soul, particularly in a relationship. This power is definitely still intact in Charlotte with her radiant beauty and her love of European culture, but the more passionate manifestation of Soul had been suppressed all her life by her identification with the ascetic ideals of Isaiah and the negating guilt of Mud. The lily, the Magic Key, transformed her by allowing her to center herself instead in the flower-like beauty of her soul, rooted in the earth but part of heaven.

The Action

The dynamic of the Hero's Journey is the call of the Mothers to initiation, to a synthesis with some forgotten or neglected aspect of Being. This is the dynamic of the individuation process. The volitional self, the Hero, responds to the call. In so doing, he is given help from the Mothers in the form of the Magic Helper and the power bestowed by it. This power provides direct access to the Mothers and allows the Hero to overcome the resistance within himself, including his inhibitions and great fear of the Mothers themselves, to return to them and uncover within the greater Self that new (ancient, but forgotten) element of the Mothers that beckoned him into this initiation. This newly assimilated, ancient element becomes a boon which the Hero integrates back into his life and the lives of those who share in his return. The central dynamic then is between the Mothers of Being and the elements that resist union with them.

The central dynamic in Charlotte's story is the call of the organic feminine in her nature—primordial Being, the great source of birth, flesh and all manner of matter. This "call to adventure" is initiated by the appearance of Puck on a bright, sunny day. Isaiah, the ascetic idealist, the pristine aspirant, wants to have nothing to do with this all-too-human flesh. Hence his fear of water, his distaste for the feminine. He is horrified when he thinks that Puck is a girl. "He doesn't want to see any girls." And yet he responds to the call, because, being so desiccated and alienated from life and its vitality, he is desperate. The scene of this struggle is the heart of Charlotte, because it is there that the call of the Mothers is heard and an authentic response is possible.

Isaiah's journey leads him through many feminine elements. Like Charlotte, he is desperate. This desperation causes him to follow after Puck, even though (or secretly because?) he thinks Puck is a girl, and to accept the gift of the lily, the Magic Key to open the soul to the feminine source. Heroically, he dives with Puck into the waters. What desperation *that* must have taken, considering that in his home he had two drains to keep his favorite room absolutely dry! And sure enough, it *is* too pleasurable! He *does* get into trouble, because there, under the forbidden waters, Mud would drown him in the clutches of its tentacles of guilt. It is only with the power of Soul that Isaiah is able to save himself from this consuming morass of moral negativity. Overcoming Mud, Isaiah is freed. Hence the first transformation represented by the fact that the Hero finds himself in his meadow, now paradisical and green, alive with springtime and new life forms.

In Part 2, Charlotte, now a new synthesis of Hero, Helper, and transformed Monster energy, is drawn further to the Mothers where she must confront a huge diseased blob of organic corruption. As Isaiah with all his religious rationalizations, she had been trained and aspired herself to avoid that very undifferentiated ooze. But the primeval Mothers *are* her. They are the forbidden aspect of her own feminine essence, horrible in the shadows.

There are at least three levels of meaning in this Supreme Ordeal, all having to do with the relationship of spirit and matter. The first level of meaning is philosophical, not usually significant in the mystery of the psyche, but having definite psychological consequences because the Hero Isaiah is devoted to the Christian tradition of asceticism. The organic, diseased blob represents the material reality that is emotionally posited as the fall from the ideal of spirit. The world of matter is the degeneration of spirit. The psychological consequence of this religious ideal is well represented in the Dream. If you create the ideal (Isaiah), you will posit the horror of its opposite (noisome blob of matter).

Being "good" within this ideal is the compulsion to transcend matter. The failure to be "good" means to fall into matter (Mud) and, worse, into disease (the blob). This blob of disease lay beneath the guilt of Mud. If Charlotte did not maintain her ascetic control, she would become a huge sore with no shape—disintegration, decay, rot. In her real life journey, her crisis had been precipitated by the fact that her mother—despite Christian Science beliefs—had recently died of cancer. This had filled her with disgust and revulsion (at the Mothers) and had traumatized her beliefs in the power of the Christian Science discipline, of which her mother had been the source and ideal practitioner. This was truly the antithesis of the strivings of Isaiah and the ultimate antipathy of a rigid philosophical-religious view.

This Supreme Ordeal was to put her in touch again with the truth of Being. There was yet another level to the entity in the Supreme Ordeal, the benign level of the Mothers of Being. Her horror was directed at all that is moist, indefinable and organic. From the point of view of the dried-up asceticism of Isaiah, these elements were confused with noisome decay. And the whole constituted a fear of her own origins, her own sex and sexual organs, which are truly of the Mothers.

In every way she struggled to avoid the *Mother that she is*. But Puck, the green heart and soul of nature, saved the day by guiding her through this organic manifestation of her fear so that she could transcend the complex, the opposition to the Mothers. With the help of Puck and the power of the Soul, the Magic Key, she makes her way through this primal ooze. At the end of the Supreme Ordeal she is pushed through a "small black hole into a bright, warm space," the very core of the Mothers, the womb which is her source. At last she comes to rest, now reborn back into the female essence from which she comes and which she is.

The reward for this initiation is Violet, a crescent moon—all the feminine qualities that she had lost. Now she is restored to the "moon qualities" that make her whole. When the sun shines upon Violet at the top of the mountain, her reward, her new Self, becomes blindingly brilliant—a star.

The elements of this Dream are particular to the constellation of Charlotte's psyche, but their meaning is significant far beyond her individual circumstances. It expresses in a particularly poignant way the dilemma of the modern woman who would rise in a man's world, but who in doing so loses her roots in her own feminine essence. The Dream also portrays the way Westerners get lost between spirit and matter; how our over-adherence to either of them perverts our relationship to the other.

In essence, the Mothers of Being have called Charlotte (as they are calling all of humankind) to find a new synthesis of spirit and matter through the truth of the heart. This new synthesis enables her to become whole as a woman and therefore as a truly holy person.

A Love Story: The Archetype of the Union of Opposites

The archetypal plot form of the Love Story expresses the union of opposites, which is the second principle of transformation. The archetypal opposites are expressed in the primal relationship of the masculine and feminine elements. They are the image of all dualities, and the archetype relates the saga of all that is incomplete without its opposite.

I first became aware of this archetype as I sat and watched a performance of the Ramayana before the temple gates during my first visit to Bali. In its characters and action, so fundamental to all love stories, I felt the constellation of the whole Self and the process by which contending opposites are transformed into a unity of complements.

The archetype has four character elements: the Hero, the Heroine, the Monster and the Nature Spirit. It has five action elements: the Hero and Heroine are together; the Monster distracts the Hero and abducts the Heroine; the Nature Spirit appears to the Hero and/or the Heroine, brings awareness of what has happened and presents a Magic Implement; with the power of the Magic Implement the Monster is overcome; and the Hero and Heroine are reunited.

In a way different from the Hero's Journey, the Love Story archetype constellates the universe of the Self. The whole is given as a primordial, original, undifferentiated union of masculine and feminine elements. The Hero is the essential male image. He is the embodiment of *yang*, or the active principle. He is the pure thrust forward; will transformed into action. He represents every characteristic that is considered masculine: reason, will, action, thinking, sensation, force, determination. For the Shivaists of India, this principle is eloquently represented by the phallus, the Shiva lingum.

The Heroine is the essential female image. She is the embodiment of *yin*, or the receptive principle. She is that which receives, waits, allows, that which is open. She is the feeling and intuitive side, the aspect that can truly know and manifest nature and the divine. For the Shivaists she is symbolized as a *yoni*, the feminine counterpart of the phallus.

The Monster is the dysfunction in the pure relationship, flow and harmony of active and receptive energies. It is the neurotic controller who wants to take over, destroy all receptivity and run the scene according to its own lights. It is the manipulative, controlling, destructive ego. It usurps the *yang* energy for its own power-oriented purposes and is thus sometimes described as double *yang*. It usurps further power by obliterating the feminine aspect of receptivity to what is so without and within. Out of fear, lack of trust in the Mothers of Being, the Monster must control circumstances to its own ends. This fear is the Monster's vulnerability. Compulsively, the Monster manipulates everything, and the egotism with which it directs this control wreaks havoc all around.

When the feminine receptivity is clarified and its potential freed to its rightful union with the active energy, the Monster can no longer exist. It is not that the *yin* principle is an enemy of the Monster, but if receptivity is cleared and given its rightful place the double-*yang* of the Monster is neutralized.

The Mothers manifest as the Nature Spirit, representing the force of nature—individuation—which is trying to bring these two opposites together into one complementary whole. The Spirit accomplishes this by bringing to one or both lovers awareness of the true situation and presenting some synchronistic and relevant power by which the separation can be overcome and the opposites restored to their natural balance. Again, the Mothers of Being desire this unity. They work through the Spirit to overcome that which is set against this ultimate union.

The inner meaning of the archetype is the alchemical figure of the union of the masculine and feminine elements of the psyche. For this reason I sometimes call it the "androgyne archetype." It is usually passed off as an objective love story between two individuals. This is partly because of the chronic objectification of all archetypal material in our time, but also because in the last two millennia, the patriarchal, Judeo-Christian ethos has suppressed the idea of the androgyne altogether. The two sexes in one being has been presented as imperfect, distorted, as hermaphrodite or homosexual. But the true androgyne has a far more important sense: the human being who has realized and balanced within himself the full possibilities of receptive and active modes of being. This realization is the highest development a human being can reach. It is also the condition for spiritual wholeness, the realization of the One, of God. This is why I call such a condition of being "the divine androgyne."

Tom's Dream

Tom was a Boston intellectual with a degree in mathematics. He was married, a real-estate salesman and white-water sportsman. He was also a transvestite, though he prefers the less prejudicial term "cross-dresser." In his *femme* persona, he is well known as the head of a national organization for cross-gender exploration. There follows an unedited transcript of his improvised psychodrama of the Dream he created and performed in the Love Story Process.

(Tom wears a black outfit. He stands in the middle as the Witness, whom he calls *Whatnot*. He moves to his right and holds a book as the Hero, *Aristotle*. As *Demeter,* the Heroine, he steps to the left and wears a big hat. He steps back and wears a black Arab robe as *Oxamander,* the Monster. And he steps forward as *Artemis,* the Nature Spirit.)

WHATNOT: Good evening. Tonight we are about to see a play about a person who has gained, lost, and may be in the process of regaining the unification of two important beings. I would like to introduce you to these two beings, as they were when they were united. Their names are Aristotle and Demeter.

ARISTOTLE: (holds a book) Hello, my name is Aristotle, and I've lived on this earth a good many years. I'm quite content with the kinds of attributes I consider myself fortunate to possess. Among those are creativeness, decisiveness, a sense of the heroic, and knowledge. I also have a great deal of reverence for a sister whose name is Demeter. And I would like you to meet her.

DEMETER: Hello. My name is Demeter. And I am the other part of the principals in this play. I am nurturing, giving and wise. I've lived for a good number of years with my brother, Aristotle. We lived in great harmony and unity for many years, until we met an outsider...who caused us to dissolve our union. And I would like to let the audience know something about this Monster.

OXAMANDER: (Monster growls and stands with shoulders tensed up) My name is Oxamander. That is, Oxamander, and I am a Monster. My power is beyond the ken of mere men. Even gods are reduced to nothing before me. I can disrupt; I can break; and I can destroy. I revel in it. (laughs sinisterly) I was given the privilege of wrecking and destroying a beautiful union here. And I would like to tell you how I did that.

Over the hero I cast a spell. I made him forget his true power. I made him reject his maleness and become sort of a non-entity in the world of men. He is called Aristotle. (laughs sinisterly) And from his sister, the divine Demeter, I made a silly, frivolous woman, one who cared not for the better things in life, but more about her trousseau, her superficialities and the mundanities of daily living. Without further ado, I'd like to introduce you to *my* Aristotle. (laughs)

ARISTOTLE: (very dottily, with a fake English accent) Hello, good friends. I am Aristotle, wise and to some extent disappointed with the values that I have cherished so much in my life. My life has been dedicated to learning about the world. And through that knowledge, to give love. Some years ago I lost my sister, who was very close to me. She went on a different road, through some mysterious forces I have yet to fathom. I am looking for her, and I'm hopeful...perhaps...something will come to allow us to be together again.

DEMETER: (speaks like a superficial, silly Englishwoman) Hello. (chuckles) My name is Demeter, and I've just come from the salon where I had my hair done, my nails done, and I went to my favorite shop and bought the most delectable frock for the summer. I revel in the superficialities of life. They are to me the essence. All the other things that I lived by many years ago are passe. And to boot, I've disassociated myself from that *bore* of a brother, Aristotle. He's never been able to come to grips with his masculinity since I've left him. Poor fellow. Once in a while, I have a yearning to see the poor chap. Maybe we shall meet again.

ARISTOTLE: I am going into the forest to look for a solution to this dilemma. I want to see my Demeter as I know I think she was.

ARTEMIS: (stands with arms upstretched) Oh, Aristotle, come into the Forest Primeval. I am Artemis, the spirit of nature, and I have a magic weapon through which you will be able to reunite yourself with Demeter, your wayward sister. And you will also be able to defeat the cause of your dissolution, Oxamander the Monster.

I give to you this stone called Sophia. In the embodiment of Sophia are three principles. They are: Know thyself. Love thyself. And be kind to others. With this magical weapon, you now have the power to defeat the Monster.

ARISTOTLE: (clutching his book) My God, what an experience! To meet Artemis and to be given the magical stone, Sophia! Oh, dear Sophia, tell me how I can best use you to reunite myself with Demeter. Give me a clue. Give me a clue. Give me a clue.

DEMETER: Ah. I've finally come to grips with my reality. The superficialities of my life these past years have been helpful, but have caused also great problems. I am not as happy as I was. I have received word from Aristotle that he has a magic stone which will help us in reunification. He has given it to me to hold, and I feel some change taking place. (her voice modifies to softer tones)

ARTEMIS: Oh, Woman, return to the Forest Primeval whose divine mother, the Earth, you have forgotten yourself to be.

Your forgottenness is great, but the peril of your beloved is greater still. He has lost his manliness and, further, he has lost his godliness. When the stone Sophia has freed him from the spell of the evil Monster, he will remember you. Then, and only then, can you give him to remember that he too is a god.

DEMETER: Your truth shall prevail, Sister. It would be good for Ari and myself to come back together and, united, we can defeat this so-called Monster, Oxamander.

OXAMANDER: (laughs) Did you hear that, audience? Did you hear that? (laughs) Here are two loyal, subjugated persons who want to demolish *me*, Oxamander. Is that not comical? Yet they say they have a magical stone with infinite powers to destroy me. I would like to know how they intend to do that to me, the invincible Oxamander, who can inflict pain, who can go through various stages in one's Anima and Animus and get the negative kernals at work on them. Me, Oxamander, master caster of spells. I would like to know what will be happening. Ah ha ha ha ha.

Hark! I hear...I hear phrases that are death knells to me. They are saying, know thyself. To thine own self be true. Love thyself. Through that knowledge you can love others and be sure of your way. Be kind to others. Let them live through your being and divine wisdom.

Yes, Yes! I give up! You may have your way. I will return you to your source, your beloved. I will give you all powerful knowledge to rule the world.

ARISTOTLE: Demeter, Beloved, at last the Monster is overwhelmed.

OXAMANDER: (aside) Ah hah! They do not see the true secret of my power. I shall prevail.

DEMETER: Aristotle, my hero, it is a trick. The spell of the Monster is breaking, but you must remember my divine nature. Love yourself beyond, know yourself beyond, and you will break the evil spell. Great God! Great One! Remember!

ARISTOTLE: Through your love I remember, Beloved, I remember. I am the all powerful creator, strong, force...

OXAMANDER: This knowing will kill me. It will defeat me. It will force me to leave the minds of Aristotle and of Demeter. Oh ... farewell ... farewell ....

ARISTOTLE: Hello. This is Aristotle. I come to share with you great news. I am reunited with Demeter, and I have defeated Oxamander. He has taught me some very hard lessons. And through these I have been able to now reform a unified pattern to my life, one which will give me and my dear Demeter heightened awareness and a life that can be of use to others.

DEMETER: Dear friends, I want to share with you the joyous experience of reunification with Aristotle, my brother. I have seen the error of my ways, the frivolity, the superficiality of a life pattern that leads nowhere. In truth, it is better to be reunited with my brother than to go off on my frivolous course, and not ever achieve the kind of contentment and happiness I know I can find with him.

WHATNOT: This is the Witness speaking. I thank you for being such a good audience and sharing with us this marvelous story. What you have seen is an attempted enactment of a most wonderful process, one in which some of the key forces in life are affected. For this process, I wish to honor the person who fomented this magical experience. He has worked with great heart and heavy hand sometimes in making this transformation possible. And as a Witness I feel honored to thank him. Thank you all and good night.

The Characters

The characters in Tom's Dream reflect his largely Greek heritage. But they have their own dream logic, independent of, yet definitely informed by, the Greek mythology from which their names are drawn.

Due to the fact that Tom is a cross-dresser, there was a particular drama involved in his Dream, and his Love Story is more complex than that of the usual Neophyte—and endlessly fascinating. In his real life, he already suffered from the split between his female and male personalities. The Monster is inextricably tied up in these personalities, so it was important that the Hero and Heroine of his Dream be created independently of this overt and somewhat pathological duality. A fresh start was necessary in order to find the internal Hero and Heroine who figured in his inner movement toward individuation.

It was very significant that the Hero and Heroine were both gods and that they were brother and sister. The Monster, Oxamander, had cast a spell over them so that they were reduced to trivial human beings. They were preoccupied with superficial exterior matters and did not even recognize each other. The Monster's work was *to exteriorize and trivialize both aspects of Tom, thus turning the internal drive of individuation into an external ritual of compulsive cross-dressing.* This externalization and all the distraction it entails concealed from Tom the real issue of internal realization and alchemical marriage.

Oxamander was constantly weakening Aristotle, the masculine side. This became apparent in the exercises of the Process in which the Hero was created. In every way, Tom kept denying and confining his physical masculinity, which was hard to do, as Tom is a large and virile man.

In sharing his past, it became clear that the Monster had used all sorts of devices to weaken Tom's masculine side. Long ago he had developed a fear of being assertive, a fear that is often found in women. Oxamander was constantly telling Tom that he was weak, ineffectual and a failure. He was always putting Tom in situations in which he was negatively dominated by women. And the strongest woman of all, Tom's *femme* personality—a lady awesome in her matronly self-assurance—wreaked havoc in his life as a man. "Her" flowering in the world was incidentally destroying his marriage and his focus on his work as a businessman. At times it looked as if Oxamander were using this *femme* personality to destroy Tom completely.

In the original guided fantasy, Aristotle appeared as an ideal man in his prime: "powerful, yet graceful, with thick hair, protective and intelligent." His mission was "to teach, to carry *form* to others, through objectivity and the application of knowledge." Tom was in fact also such a man, except for the work of Oxamander who usurped his manhood, causing him to deny it in every possible way, including cutting off all of his body hair, confining the space in which he allowed physical movement and cramming his genitals into girdles. Hence the emasculated, dotty Aristotle portrayed in the performance with all of his books, scrolls and charts.

The name of the Monster is Oxamander, a combination of "ox" and "man"—two bluntly masculine syllables that accurately express the double *yang* of the Monster. Clearly, the denial of the masculine side had submerged that energy, and this denied energy was negating Tom in return. The classical nature of the Monster is that it is the energy of the Mothers denied and turned destructively back upon the denier.

The Heroine, Demeter, was the Mother of Earth in Greek mythology. In Tom's guided fantasy she was a beautiful and poised woman, but when Tom portrayed her during the presentations of the Heroine—which he did, of course, with great artfulness—she was trivialized into a frivolous *femme mondaine* concerned only with clothes and jewels. Oxamander's project with her was to prevent her real femininity from touching and perhaps releasing Aristotle from his spell.

The Nature Spirit was Artemis, who in Greek Mythology is the Goddess of the Forest and Wild Animals, of insight and feminine power. Tom's portrayal of Artemis was truly essential, without caricature. One could see the real serenity of Tom's feminine side, which, if integrated, would be the source of great strength and complementary power to his manliness.

The Magic Implement was powerful indeed. It was a stone named "Sophia," which in Greek means wisdom. The power of this wisdom was the key to the entire drama: "know thyself, love thyself, be kind to all." This was the key to releasing the power of the Monster and allowing the true masculinity and femininity to come together in the androgynous state. During the creation of the Nature Spirit in the session, Artemis elaborated upon this wisdom by telling Tom that he could unite his two separate personalities by the following: "Know the two, and you shall know the One. Love the two and you shall become the One." These are incredibly powerful propositions; the epitome of archaic and eternal wisdom—truly *sophia*.

The Action

In the Love Story, the return to the Mothers is very specific. The Neophyte is conveyed to the divine source, out of which come forth the opposites, masculine and feminine. The Mothers, as the Origins, are also the force that draws the Hero and Heroine to return to the primordial oneness out of which they came. The Hero, or active self, succumbs to the temptations of the Monster, asserts himself, and pursues some distraction or other. The Heroine, left to her own devices, falls prey to the inhibiting fiend who would bring everything under his control. Control by the ego constitutes the elimination of the feminine principle which is in essence receptive— the very opposite of control.

This divisiveness is intolerable to the Mothers. They send forth the Nature Spirit who helps the Hero become aware of his plight and of his loss. The Spirit empowers the lovers with whatever is necessary to outwit or otherwise overcome the Monster. This the Hero does (sometimes assisted by the Heroine) with the magic powers from the Mothers, who rejoice at the release of the feminine and its reunification with the masculine. This is the alchemical union. Again, there is disorder called back into order by the Mothers and their instrument, the archetype.

In Tom's story, the Monster has brought about a double fall. The Hero and Heroine represent the divine state of union. They are One, both gods. Oxamander casts a spell over them, and they forget. First they forget their divine nature, they lose their union, and they lose their power as separate human beings. Aristotle becomes a dotty, ineffectual old man fussing about his charts and books. Demeter becomes a silly *femme mondaine* who cares for nothing but her hats and baubles. Their relationship and their true nature is but a distant memory.

Aristotle is the mind of man overwrought and divorced from its roots in the earth. Experiencing the aridity of his life, he begins to feel nostalgia for his long lost lover-sister, a longing that sends him on his quest. This gives the Mothers their chance, and they send him the blue-eyed goddess Artemis, who gives him the stone of human wisdom, Sophia. This stone grounds him with what he needs for self-remembering, "Know thyself," and for reuniting with his feminine nature, "Love thyself and be kind to others."

Demeter, too, now disillusioned with her state, is awakened by Artemis, and together, with the help of the stone, they remember who they are, thereby neutralizing the false but powerful Oxamander. It takes Aristotle a little longer to return to his origins, as he is divorced from the Mothers and lost in his mind. But finally, with the help of the stone, Artemis succeeds in bringing him back to an awareness of his true divine nature, so that he is once again able to be reunited with nature and the Divine Earth, his sister. This we understand to be the desire of the Mothers of Being.

There are three stages to Tom's Self-remembering. The first is retrieval from his state as a de-natured intellectual. The second is his reawakening to his relationship to his sister, the Earth. The force of this feminine element (the need of Mother Earth to be recognized) is so powerful that when Oxamander casts the spell over Aristotle which causes everything to be seen and dealt with in exterior and superficial terms, the feminine force actually overpowers Tom and takes over his identity. The authentic drive from the Mothers to assimilate the feminine principle gets perverted into the compulsion to *be* a woman. The third stage of Self-remembering is Tom's own divine state, his divine being, the ultimate union of man's mind with God. These three levels of Self-remembering raise Tom from the humiliation of a split identity and the life as a compulsive cross-dresser to the possibility of true androgynous wholeness, whose boon is the ultimate mystical knowing.

This Love Story was particularly beautiful because it was between two characters of great significance to our civilization: Demeter, the goddess of the Earth, and Aristotle, the mind of man. The relationship between the two was even closer because they were brother and sister. Their love story is the ultimate love story between man and nature. It is precisely because of the split between his (Apollonian) mind and the (Dionysian) earth that humankind is in such grave peril of destroying itself. And it is because of the excessively *yang* or patriarchal mind, represented by Oxamander, that this split has taken place. The stone, with its powerful wisdom, "Know the two and you shall know the One," is truly the antidote to the polarization of all opposites. Its other power, "Know thyself, Love thyself, Be kind to all," is the wisdom of all healing. Tom's Love Story transcends Dream and becomes Myth, because it relates the essential story of Western civilization itself.

The Central Dynamic and the Naming of the Unnamed Gods

In both of the archetypal plot forms the central dynamic is between Being and the disruptive elements contained within it—between the whole and the dysfunctional part. It looks like good and evil, but the Monster transcends mere morality—it is unspeakably clever and uses good as well as evil to its disruptive ends. Look at Charlotte's hero, Isaiah. Is he good or evil? He has lived a life of strict unyielding adherence to principles of goodness, but he has robbed Charlotte of her nature!

At the very root of our existence, the Origins are the Mothers, the sources of Being energy. When their order is disrupted by the wayward Monster, there is havoc. *Hubris* rules, and the Monster has his day. But then, with the full force of Nature, the Mothers send forth their ambassadors of natural will, the Magic Helpers and the Nature Spirits, and man, the pawn in between, is returned to harmony with the source. This is the stuff of the grandest tragedy and of each and every life. These are the eternal forces, the gods, of the human universe. The Dream is the "naming" of the gods that exist in the individual universe.

The character of the Monster is most significant and important in the Process. It is also the most colorful and interesting.

The Monster is the most significant because, however fun and humorous it may be, it is a symbolic expression of all that is actually self-destructive in life. Everyone has a Monster, unless the individuation process is completed—a very rare state of maturity that I myself have never come across. The fact is, most people ultimately die by the doings of their Monster. It almost never happens that someone actually dies of old age. It is rather the Monster that finds some way to destroy the person through disease or some other perpetrated dysfunction of the spirit and the organism. In this sense, the ORIGINS work is literally a matter of life and death.

The Monster is also the most important character because, dramatically speaking, it is only out of the dysfunction of order that the drama is created in the first place. What dramatic value would there be if the Hero's way were never obstructed by some negative force? Who would be interested in a Love Story in which there was no problem that arose between the lovers or nothing that threatened their unity? It is the Monster in all its hateful, dysfunctional negativity that generates the dramatic situation.

This says a great deal about what life is all about and why it is interesting. Unless we were quite differently constituted, a harmonious paradise in which nothing was amiss might be a bloodless bore.

The Monster is the transcendental force of *hubris*. The ORIGINS Process is always an experience of gradual revelation of *hubris* as the many faces and levels of the Monster appear. In many mythologies, the Monster is portrayed as having many heads. Often when you chop off one head, ten more grow back in its place. Having "beheaded" many of my own Monsters and worked with countless more created by others, I can confirm that this is psychologically accurate. There is no such thing as completely doing away with the Monster. There is always more.

Let us look deeper into the nature of *hubris* in its incarnation as the Monster.

The first characteristic of the Monster is that it hides. This is what a detective story is all about. Much of what is initially uncovered in the work is but a smokescreen emitted by the Monster to avoid discovery, because awareness is one of the truly authentic ways by which the Monster is eliminated. It thrives by directing blame away from itself and creating false issues to distract the Hero. In fact, most participants have never really known of the Monster as such until, as Novices in the CHAOS Stage, they begin the work of observing incidences of resistance.

We all know ourselves as victims. We have all been depressed, sabotaged, put down, suppressed, made inferior, repressed. But when we are asked who is the depressor, the saboteur, the repressor, we either point outward into the world or draw a blank. We have no idea. It is part of the smokescreen of the Monster to make us see ourselves only as victims while concealing the fact that we are also the victimizer who is creating the suffering in the first place. For many Neophytes, the act of taking on the role of the one who creates suffering is already a revelation, opening new vistas of self-awareness and possibilities for responsibly reowning our full power.

Another illusory aspect of the Monster is to be found in the "spell" cast by it over the other characters created in the Process. These characters are often severely distorted by the Monster. Isaiah in Charlotte's story is wizened by the excesses of his asceticism. His dry, lifeless morality is a terrible spell cast by the Monster. Aristotle and Demeter in Tom's dramatization become caricatures of their god-like realities under the influence of Oxamander.

In the portrayal of the characters in the Love Story, this distortion has a particular importance. For a man playing a woman or for a woman playing a man, the challenge is to portray a character of the opposite sex *without caricature*. Distorting the heroic aspect is "monstrous." It is easy to play a lady in drag, but what is coming across is a significant distortion of the feminine principle. Drag is the Monster masquerading as the feminine. It is quite another thing to play real femininity, and much more difficult! The more realistically a man can portray his feminine character, the more you know the man has integrated his femininity.

The distortion of the characters is another way that the Monster deflects attention away from himself. Much of the analysis of the characters has to do with determining elements that are part of the spell cast by the Monster. Very often, as in Tom's dramatization, this casting of spells figures in the action itself.

The Monster is the possibility for an authentic engagement with the Origins. In each archetype, the Monster is constellated differently and the dynamic happens in a characteristic way. In the Hero's Journey, the Monster manifests as fear of change, inhibition and the complex of fundamental fear.

DREAM: Monster in Bali.

In the Love Story, the Monster is the dysfunction in the relationship between the active and receptive aspects of the Self. But in both cases the Monster, in his negative form, holds the keys to the initiation by the Mothers, and it is the purpose of the Process, with the help of the Nature Spirit, to dispel this negative form so that the initiation can take place.

Going deeper into the actual nature of the Monster, we discover how it generates psychological pathology. The Monster is to a large degree part of the total energy of the Self. It is that aspect of the Mothers of Being that, for whatever reason, is refused. This refusal is the *hubris*. Tom has refused his masculinity. Charlotte has refused her organic femininity. *When there is negation of primal energy, that energy in turn negates the volitional self which negated it in the first place.* This the law of *hubris*, the source of neurosis and, often, of psychosis. It is also the key to transformation.

The transmutation of the Monster is a matter of uncovering the original negation of the Mothers and reowning that which rightfully belongs as part of the Self. This process is profoundly healing and constitutes the primary transformational work in the ORIGINS Process.

But who does the Monster work for? Beneath the aspect of the Monster that can be transcended, there is, I believe, a dark force that is transpersonal and truly evil. It lives and feeds on the negation of primal energy, but is not reducible to it. This dark force is part of the Mystery of the universe, and surely has as one of its chaotic goals ultimately to destroy humanity itself. Such is my conviction after years of work on personal Monsters in the Dream and collective Monsters represented in the MYTH and RITUAL Stages of the Process.

Being is the context, the "double" of the drama. It is the totality of what is portrayed in each Dream. The laws of Being always transcend the power of the Monster which, however dysfunctional it may be, nevertheless remains within the context of the whole. The whole is not portrayed as such (except as the *imago dei*). The whole is the laws that govern the archetypes themselves, the unlimited Spirit of Nature.

Insofar as the characters of the Magic Helper and the Nature Spirit are ambassadors of this totality, they represent its ultimate truth and force. This is why these Spirits of Nature have such power and strength, and why, in the full archetype, they always prevail. Within the context of the story, however, they always appear as *compensatory* against the background of the drama created by the Monster. The dysfunctional situation is created by the Monster, and the Spirits of Nature appear in order to counteract this force and restore the ultimate balance of Being.

The true heroes of civilization are those great leaders of the spirit who, through their enlightenment, transform their personal Monsters by assimilating them into divine wholeness. Only when this level of wholeness is reached can they set out to deal with the great transpersonal forces of darkness aboard in the universe.

But for whom do the great forces of darkness work?

They ultimately serve the ever-greater Being who guides the Way of all process—from the changes of the individual to the ultimate movements of the Universe. It is Being in its law of being. It is the One, eternally changing, and becoming One.

The Transformational Process in the DREAM

Transformation in the DREAM Stage is the core of the entire ORIGINS Process—both at the level of the individual (personal and performer) and at the level of that which is projected into the audience through the production. By considering this transformation in some depth, we can derive a clear idea of the effect that the training should have on the Neophyte in the process of evolving into a holy performer. The clear definition of transformation also gives us the key to understanding at a psychological level the nature of the Sacred, and therefore the essential content of Sacred Performing Art.

The methods and form of the DREAM Process grew out of my work as a therapist. Because of my affinity for the performing arts, I have naturally gravitated toward therapeutic devices involving performance expression. The DREAM Process was first developed through work with serious pathologies and psychoses; then it was adapted as a method for working out the transitions that manifest as neuroses; then it was used as a device to create greater freedom of expression for persons in general and for performers in particular.

During the years that I have been working in these areas, I have seen that the entire notion of therapy has become relative. It would be one thing if there were a well-defined ground of normalcy or health against which a figure, a profile of true pathology, could be defined. Then we would have a clear idea of what therapy was all about. The fact is, however, that the *ground itself is changing*, and much that looks like pathology is actually some aspect or other of a transition that everyone is having to make as a function of this, our time in history. For this reason, the entire notion of therapy presents many difficulties. It is impossible to determine the pathology of the figure when the ground itself is changing.

The Paradigm of the Ideal and the Paradigm of Wholeness

The change of ground may be described as a change in paradigm: from the paradigm of the *ideal* to that of the *total*. It is necessary to understand where one is on the continuum between these two paradigms before it is possible to determine that the behaviors manifested in any given case are pathological or merely a healthy adaptation to a change in the preconditions of well-being.

The paradigm of the ideal has governed the West since the time of the ancient Hebrews and Greeks. There is an ideal way of being: Through will and discipline, one grows toward that ideal by continually pruning oneself to conform to it. In Greece, this was the way of Apollo. In India this is called the way of *yoga*, the way of the will. It is the same in Islam and in Christianity. One wills to achieve a certain state or ideal way of being, and the entire development must fall in line with the direction of this will. For instance, the ideal set forth for me may be to become a good Christian, a Yale man, a fine American. Then my "progress" in life (and the degree to which I am considered pathological) is measured by how well I am able to achieve this ideal. What is ideal is "good," and this "good" exists only where there also is "bad." Thus I am compelled to love one "person" who is good and hate one "person" who is bad: God and the Devil respectively.

Freud's theory of the personality exposed the way in which the Self, operating in the paradigm of the ideal, generates psychopathology. Freud demonstrated how the pathologies of nineteenth-century Vienna all resulted from the ego attempting to fulfill itself according to norms of ideal behavior laid down by the super-ego. The problem, Freud showed, is that unbearable tensions result from the demands of the id—the itness of who we really are as a function of nature (the Mothers). Striving toward an ego-ideal always creates a Monster, because what does not serve the ego-ideal has to be rejected. And, as I have said, if you reject part of the Self it turns on you and negates you. This process, which Freud called "the return of the repressed," is precisely identical with the Monster. And the Monster—creation of the ideal—is the source of all psychopathology. Hence, the necessity of therapy.

This paradigm that strives toward an ideal and goes on creating antagonistic shadows is bankrupt. It is still the basis of our Western values, but the sense of despair and cynicism that is abroad in the world is eloquent testimony of its bankruptcy. No "ideal" works! Moreover, we have tried so hard to be what we "ought to be" that we no longer know who we are. Those who look for positive alternatives, however, see that the paradigm of the ideal is being replaced by another paradigm in a transition that is almost cataclysmic.

The paradigm of wholeness or totality is an integral part of the East. It is also akin to the spirit of Dionysus. In the modern West it has been set out by Jung with his notion of Individuation. An individuated person is not one who has achieved an ideal, but one who has successfully allowed the mysterious process of integration to unfold within and create what one uniquely is. The basic element of this process is surrender. In India, this surrender is associated with *Tantra*. One does not try to fulfill an idea; one surrenders to what is being given. One has to live with ambiguity. One has to accept loving and hating the same person at the same time. One comes to understand God and the Devil—indeed all opposites—as complementary. The Self unfolds in the process of surrendering, not by moving toward some goal. This surrender requires great trust in the wisdom of the unfolding.

The interface of these two paradigms can be seen in the Hero's Journey archetype. The paradigm of the ideal is represented by the striving Hero. He creates the Monster as the shadow of his own self-will. The ascetic Isaiah in Charlotte's dream is the apotheosis of this kind of Western Hero. The paradigm of the whole is represented by Charlotte at the end of the journey, when she has been initiated into that which gives her a new wholeness. Charlotte's reward, "Violet," with its powerful feminine capacity, does not make Isaiah more ideal, but rather rounds him out, makes him whole. Isaiah, the ideal, is transformed into a new being, a whole androgyne, in which masculine and feminine elements are integrated.

At the core of this paradigm shift is a spiritual movement of fundamental and dramatic significance. It has to do with the understanding of the center. In the paradigm of the ideal, nature and the human psyche are seen as chaotic and without an organizing center. The center has to be imposed by the ego. The ideal is thus a form of control that reflects a basic lack of trust in that center which has given forth the whole in the first place. This is why the ideal is the most basic form of *hubris* and why it always creates monstrous shadows which destroy its projects.

In the paradigm of the whole, the ego surrenders to the inherent (but often mysterious) order of the Self. This requires a profound trust in the wisdom and intrinsic jurisdiction of the center hidden in the whole by which nature, the universe itself, has been ordered for all time. The Mothers of Being are the guardians, the governors of this intrinsic order. In the ORIGINS Process their governance becomes transparent—the source of initiation and the prime mover of transformation.

The ORIGINS Process is all about transition from the paradigm of the ideal to that of the whole. That is why it is difficult to describe the Process in terms of therapy. It actually is about the ground of well-being, against which therapy is a relative matter.

Therapy has to do with "fixing" someone who has been wounded in the old paradigm. Transformation is about bringing people into configurations of wholeness and helping them—in the case of the ORIGINS Process, through the power of the archetypes—to see themselves and their "problems" in the greater context of the unfolding of the whole Self. With this new vision of the Self there is great enhancement of personal power. One is changed. This is what is meant by transformation.

Neophytes become initiates when this transformation is understood existentially and in some sense accomplished. They then become engaged in the project of creating a performance vehicle to bring an understanding of this new paradigm into a larger context in order to influence their audiences. That, as we shall see, is the purpose of the Myth and the Ritual.

Transpersonal Elements of Transformation

The entire ORIGINS Process is transpersonal in that it provides models of a new configuration of the Self and promotes optimal states of integration and wholeness.

During the training the optimal state is expressed in the ritual with which we open each session of Work. This ritual consists of an OM salutation; RAM chanted seven times in the body center, the heart center, the mind center and

again three times in the body center; and finally an OM salutation to close.
This exercise brings the group as a unit into the circle of Work, but it is also
the core of the teaching. As the Process moves on with all of its accumulating
insights, the exercise is repeated continually, its transpersonal teaching going
deeper and deeper into the consciousness of the group.

All Are One: the Mysticism of the One Sound

To begin with, the group is instructed to chant the OM and RAMs and all
other mantra in perfect unison. This is stressed with every repetition. When
the group succeeds in making one sound, a tangible mystical unison
envelopes everyone. This sound unity becomes the ongoing symbol of the
unity of the group. In the stages of the Process that follow the DREAM, this
unity is crucial. Each person has to balance his receptivity to the group and
his active participation in it. This is part of the overall training in the
mysticism of surrender.

The OM salutation is particularly significant here. OM is the timeless
sound symbol of the One. As the training proceeds, the Neophytes are
coming to understand in ever greater depth the nature of this One. They
come into the group with individual problems and situations that make them
feel isolated from others. In the course of the DREAM, it becomes apparent and
then obvious that all the little dramas of individual lives are actually part of
one great drama. Everyone is involved in this same drama. In fact, we are all
one person living out this drama together. This growing awareness brings
more and more meaning to the repetitions of the OM. Bowing from the waist
and folding the hands in a position of prayer during the OM becomes an act
of honoring the magnificence of this one Divine person that we all are and
the poignance of its unfolding drama.

The Three Centers

This One human being has three realities, three centers: the physical, the
emotional/spiritual, the mental. Here again, the teaching with regard to
these centers deepens as the training proceeds. To understand this teaching,
it is important to understand the configuration of these centers in the
paradigm of the ideal and in the paradigm of the whole.

In the pathology of the *ideal* paradigm, the energy of the body center
tends to be blocked. The breathing does not reach down into the belly. The

body armor is thick, enclosing the body in tensions. The sexual energy is suppressed. In the heart center, the feeling and emotion tend to be blocked, with the result that the capacity for open and loving care is shut down. The energy of these two centers is largely suppressed or repressed. The mind center, where the ideal is generated and supported by the belief system, attempts to monitor the entire personality. Mind is thus cut off from its grounding in feeling and the physical dynamic.

The profile of the centers in the ideal paradigm is an overworked mind center blocking the body and heart centers. This is also the profile of *hubris*. The blocked energy does not cease to exist; rather, as we have seen, it is turned against the pure energies in the form of the Monster and militates against the Hero. Anyone who sees the powerful force of the Monsters as they are portrayed in the psychodramatic presentations can see that they embody tremendous energy.

The configuration of the *totality* paradigm is one in which the energy of each center is free and clear. The three centers functioning together are capable of a flexible harmony in any situation. The constant repetition of the RAM exercise provides an ever-deepening reinforcement of wholeness by constantly drawing attention to it. The exercise also works on opening the centers by bringing breath into them and stimulating them with the vibration of the mantram. This attention, focusing and vibrating help to release the three energies, to clarify the kinds of experience each represents and to demonstrate how they are when they function in harmony. Subliminally, these repetitions center the Neophyte in himself and in the new paradigm. It is like programming the body and the subconscious. The ritual of the RAMs in the three centers is the most important exercise in the Process, and it is also the one that is practiced most frequently.

This programming of the body with the essence of wholeness, supported by the basic transformational work in the DREAM, is intended to rectify the pathology in the configuration of the ideal.

Yin/Yang Balance

In the Love Story Training there is presented a transpersonal theme having to do with the balance of *yin* and *yang*. The *yin* quality is that which is associated with the feminine: the earthy, the feeling, the intuitive. In essence it is the receptive element. This is what allows us to receive what is given by the givens of life on this earth. It is also that which allows us to receive the Divine. The transmutation of the Monster allows this receptivity to open to the Divine.

The *yang* or active capacity has to be freed as well. This is the power to act in a pure way, assertiveness. Many women are afraid of this power in particular because they are conditioned to believe that it is aggressive. When this activity is not in balance with a corresponding receptivity—that is, when it is in the power of the Monster—it gets incapacitated, distracted or hyped-up into control and manipulation. The interaction with the Spirit of Nature provides awareness of the dysfunctional aspect and clarifies the energy by virtue of the Magic Implement.

In both trainings one is called upon to explore receptivity and activity and to refine their balance in many capacities. In order to achieve the much heralded "one sound" in mantra the group must chant in perfect unison. This means that each person must be receptive to the pitch and intensity of the sound made by the group and must actively bring the voice into the unison. This is stressed with each repetition of mantra. In other exercises, a Neophyte must receive the perceptions of the others with complete open-ness and in turn speak with complete forthrightness. This theme of balance is thematic throughout the Love Story Training. At the end, there is assigned a meditation exercise to permit the Neophyte to carry on working toward balance in ever fuller and more enduring ways.

When these active and receptive capacities are completely freed, or even momentarily freed, one can experience what it is to move and be moved at the same time. This is a state of pure grace and an experience of utter poise, bliss. As one continues to perfect these active and receptive qualities and the subtle sense of being in pure balance, the mystical harmony of the sublime unity begins to reveal itself. And continuing with such work, through the practice of Tai Chi, for instance, one comes to understand what is meant in the Taoist tradition by "the Way" or "the One."

The Alchemical Transmutation of the Monster

Alchemy is the ancient and medieval science of transmuting base metals into gold and the quest for an elixir of life. In Jung's magnificent works on alchemy, he shows that the alchemists were actually involved in perfecting the process of individuation and turning it into a science. During the Middle

Ages, because of the censure of the Church, this inquiry had to be concealed under the guise of the ancient science of matter. The metaphorical meaning of alchemy is clear: turning a lower form and quality of being into one which allows life to be experienced in its highest form. Gold is wholeness, and the elixir of life is the blood of the Mothers of Being. This alchemy is the basic work of the DREAM.

Another way of saying this is that the work of the DREAM is to overcome the pathology due to the old configuration of the three centers and to experience the Self through the new configuration of the centers. The key for this is the transmutation of the Monster. This transmutation has three steps:

• *Dropping the dysfunctional form.* The monstrous form is identified, consciously expressed, and, through the devices of the Process, summarily or eventually dropped.

• *Integrating the freed energy into the totality.* The physical and emotional energy held in the Monster form is freed and released to be integrated into the power available to the whole person.

• *The destructive power becomes healing.* That which was negated by the ideal and thus negating the ideal now benignly serves the whole. What was saying NO *to* the essence is now protecting and energizing the whole and saying NO *for* the sake of the essence.

The Authentic Methods for Transmuting the Monster

In the psychodramatic portrayal of the battle with the Monster, I always instruct the Neophytes to add the following detail: the Hero initially forgets about the Magic Implement and attempts to overcome the Monster by force. Translated existentially, force means trying to overpower the ego-Monster by will, by discipline, by forceful resistance of any kind. That is the "normal" way of dealing with the Monster. The fact of the matter is, you cannot fight the affects of ego with more affect. You must go to the cause. Anger, fear, greed, lust—none of these forms of ego can be controlled morally. That is fighting the Monster with monstrous tactics. It may stop the affect, but it does not touch the cause. It may work as discipline, but it does not work as transformation. If you look at the fairy tales, the Monster is always too powerful. If you look at life you also see that it is too powerful. The futility of force is expressed in the Biblical phrase, "Resist not evil." If you fight the Monster with negative force, you actually feed the energy of resistance.

The essence of transmutation is to surrender to the Monster with awareness and then to deal with it at another, more subtle level. Often there has to be some way of tricking or outwitting the Monster.

Of all the subtle methods for dealing with the Monster, I have found the most authentic and effective general antidotes to be awareness, expression, catharsis and Self-love. Antidotes to the particular character of each Monster are found in the unique powers of each Magic Implement.

Awareness

The essence of surrendering is to see the Monster for what it is. This is very difficult because, as I have said, the Monster is constantly disguising and rationalizing itself as something else and sending out smokescreens and illusions. The most frequent trick of the Monster is blaming, to cause the person to see himself as the victim of the circumstances of life and to blame something or someone exterior to himself as the victimizer. The awareness in the Process has to bring sharply into view the way in which the person is himself the victimizer.

Such awareness is provided by a very exciting exercise called "Monster on the Stand": Each Neophyte performs his Monster as the group and I pose questions that call upon the Monster to identify himself and his work. Real awareness is *not* intellectualizing and making objective appraisals or criticisms of the self. As I said, these are the propensity of the Monster to masquerade as the judge. Judgment, no matter how intellectual, is not awareness at all. Awareness is simply and authentically seeing what is so about the self against the Self.

Awareness is greatly served by two other factors in the work of transmutation: expression in general, and catharsis and exaggeration in particular.

Expression: Catharsis and Exaggeration

In the DREAM Stage, most of the techniques include some form of expression. As you have seen, expression is an antidote to repression, suppression and, in a deeper way, depression. To express is to allow. Transmutation requires allowing what was unmanifest to be manifest in some apparent form so that it can come forth and be brought into awareness. New information about the Self is an initiation and always serves wholeness. When newly discovered energies are expressed in some form, it is possible to generate a greater integration of the Self.

In 1970 I was going through the tribulation of birthing a new Self after my first deep experiences of life and the pursuit of understanding in India. In the year after my return, I had severe anxiety attacks and was in therapy with a famous Jungian analyst, Dr. Gerhard Adler. Each week, he had me draw that anxiety. By analyzing these drawings, I gradually climbed on the heads of the many Monsters, right up out of anxiety into a new understanding of the Self. Drawing the Monster gives a form to a shadow entity that one hardly even knew existed. I experienced an amazing demonstration of the power of this sort of art expression, the benefits of which everyone in the DREAM Stage gets to share. Drawing or painting the characters or their emblems always brings up a fresh grasp of the new aspect of the Self that they symbolize.

Of course the main expressive technique is dramatic presentation. There are three kinds: simple performance—presentation of the characters; the psychodramatic enactment of the Dream; and other dramatization techniques used to deal with specific problems that arise. If someone cannot resolve a conflict through the psychodrama, occasionally I will use "psychotheatrics," a technique in which other members of the group take all the parts, and the Neophyte directs them through the crisis, often with my help and the help of the group. This strengthens the objectivity of the Witness and allows for a solution to be worked out using objective components.

The third expressive form is movement. Bringing an unconscious character into physical manifestation provides a level of expression that serves the Witness and allows the Neophyte to assimilate this character. This is important in enacting the Monster, the Supreme Ordeal, or the masculine or feminine self. If one portrays with totality that which one fears most, he quickly realizes that there is nothing to fear.

When the immaculate Charlotte came up with the diseased blob, I had her act out this blob by lying on the floor and writhing like the mass she saw in her Supreme Ordeal. It was dramatically irksome for her, but as she became more relaxed with it, a definite change began happening in her. If something can be expressed by the body, it can be allowed fully into awareness and can be assimilated by the Self. This is the healing/teaching principle in movement and theatrical expression.

The critical moments of catharsis built into both trainings take place in the evocation of the Monster, the psychodrama of the confrontation with the Monster and, in the Hero's Journey, the Supreme Ordeal.

As an example, in both trainings, the Monster is evoked in part by a bio-energetic process in which the NO-saying is expressed in a cathartic way. Resulting tensions are surveyed and then exaggerated. The maximal exaggeration of these body tensions, formed by hyperventilating, elicits an explosive catharsis of negative rage and power which is exorcised in what we call the Monster Dance.

This explosion of negative (and heretofore negated) power allows the actual body and emotional energy that is pent-up in the Monster to be released and embodied. The Self is then able to reown the power. The uptight energy withheld in the musculature is released back into the body, and the suppressed energy of the heart is released back into the heart. This work is complementary to the opening of the body and heart centers.

Along with embodiment and expression, the freeing of energy and awareness are greatly served by exaggerating the Monster. If there is a subtle voice telling me that what I am doing in life is not worthwhile, I normally just assume it is so and feel put down. But if I can bring this voice up into a cathartic expression and exaggerate it totally, the situation is dramatically altered. I look in a mirror and make the "accusation" to myself with great feeling and appropriate exaggerated bodily expression. It is also usually very funny. Becoming aware of this Monstrous aspect of myself, seeing that it *is* myself, allows me to take responsibility for it. Usually I can then drop it because it is so ridiculous, whereas the sneaking way in which it was masquerading as my own "objective appraisal" of myself was impossibly elusive and difficult to detect.

I tell the Neophytes to remember this exaggeration technique and to use it at any time they are feeling particularly bad about themselves. Usually the Monster is exerting a lot of energy. If they can own that energy and its message, it is possible to drop the dysfunctional form with a good laugh and reown the freed energy into the totality.

Self-love

The principle of YES that came to me in my mystical experience when I was thirty is the guiding light of all healing and transformation. The basic tenet of wholeness is that whatever is of the Self is to be honored. Self-love is the truly transformative element. The appropriate attitude toward oneself is like a loving mother or a doting lover. Self-love is the catalyst by which awareness opens into integration. This is why the basic attitude of the entire process is YES. This YES is the actualization of Self-love.

The Monster has to be seen, expressed and then loved as part of the whole. Only then does it lose its autonomous force. This aspect of Self-love is to me the essence of the Christian practice of forgiveness. Forgiveness is not just "pardoning"; it is seeing beneath the judgmental level of "fault" and "wrongness" into the true, essential innocence of the Self, the Christ which is the manifestation of God. Of course one can only achieve this level of Self-love when one learns how to forgive others; that is, to see beneath what they do into the essential innocence of the greater Self that all humanity is.

The Magic Implement

The final authentic method for transforming the Monster is the use of the Magic Implement. This power is unique in each case. Its derivation and role is one of the real miracles in the training. In the Process, it is always derived *before* the Monster is created. And synchronistically, when the Monster does make its appearance, the Magic Implement is in fact the key. This is another of many wondrous things about the two archetypes: the Self is so constellated through them that the antidote comes forth before the pathology or its figure, the Monster, is manifest.

I usually help each Neophyte arrive at a real, working understanding of how the power actually works in his case. For instance, Charlotte's Magic Implement, "Magic Key," was a lily that was found in the mud ("Mud," remember, was also the name of her Monster). This lily empowered Charlotte by bringing into focus the real value of the energy of Soul—of love, of poetry, of beauteous expressiveness. Charlotte was richly and amply endowed with these abilities. These real values were an authentic catalyst to the negativity of her moral Monster and her ascetic Hero. I encouraged her to keep a lily around her in order to be reminded of the ascendant value of the "soul" over and above the values of the very masculine world in which she moves.

These devices, powers and attitudes are the catalytic agents for authentic transmutation of the Monster. They are elements introduced into the scene that actually alter the circumstance so that the dysfunctional form can be dropped and the essential energy can be integrated into the totality. The Magic Implement is always the subtle catalyst by which the Monster can be tricked and his power transformed.

The Alchemical Formulae of Transformation

Alchemical transformation proceeds according to definite laws. The two archetypal plot forms express the two fundamental laws of transformation.

The formula of alchemical transformation in the Hero's Journey is:

Separation—Initiation—Return

The volitional self separates from the present status quo and is given a new awareness or power. The development is halted by the ego-Monster of inhibition. Overcoming the ego-Monster with the new power and assimilating the strength of the inhibiting force allows a greater volitional self to enter into the initiatory ordeal into which it is irresistibly drawn. This Initiation is a confrontation with a cataclysmic fear which conceals some essential power or insight of the Mothers of Being. Once this confrontation is completed, the secret revealed is brought back to the situation of the status quo, altering it in some essential way. This Return constitutes a transformation of the volitional self by virtue of new empowerment resulting from the Initiation. The Return represents a new level of integration and wholeness.

The Neophytes are given the Hero's Journey mandala to color or fill in with the energy of the characters and to contemplate as the form of the new whole.

The essence of transformation in the Love Story is beautifully represented in the classical Chinese *yin-yang* symbol. This symbol expresses both the original and the final unity of the masculine and feminine elements. It is used throughout the Love Story Training as a way of focusing on the highest and most balanced form of the elements, much as the OM salutation and RAMs in the three centers function as a ritual icon of the entire ORIGINS Process.

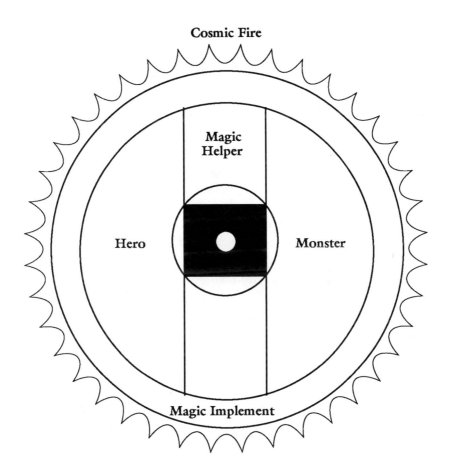

Journey Mandala

The alchemical formula of the Love Story process is:

One—Two—Three

The original Self is a pure balance of feminine-receptive and masculine-active elements. The ego-Monster causes a suppression of the receptive elements and takes over and distracts the active elements. This is the normal neurotic state of man. To redress the natural balance, the Mothers send forth their embassy, some Spirit of Nature, to bring awareness to the active self and to empower it with some grounding power from themselves. The active self uses these powers to neutralize the effect of the ego-Monster, thus freeing up the receptive capacities. With new awareness the active and receptive aspects are reunited in one whole.

The mandala of the Love Story is given to the Neophytes who fill it out with designs that represent the component characters. They use it in the meditation ritual to free their masculine and feminine sides from the overlay of negative affect from the mother and father. They also use it to ground themselves in the new wholeness represented by the mandala.

The ideal result of this alchemical process, considered as a state of human development, is called, as I have said, the divine androgyne. *Androgyne* means one who has fully freed the original capacities associated with both masculine and feminine qualities. According to Jungian thought, this is the intentionality of the entire individuation process, because all of human life is about losing, through suppression, some of these qualities and then slowly realizing them again. An authentically androgynous person is called "divine," because when these qualities are freed and balanced once again the conditions are present for totality to manifest in the psyche. This manifestation is experienced as divine. It is the internal, given answer to the basic religious question. It is the authentic experience of God from which is emitted the *imago dei.*

In its original form, the *yin-yang* symbol is always shown with a dragon moving around the periphery of the circle, representing the dynamic energy movement of *yang* and *yin* into each other. This dragon is the transmuted power of the Monster united with the energy of the Nature Spirit so that the movement around the mandala is pure and free. This is the pure form of the TAO, and the highest state of the human being.

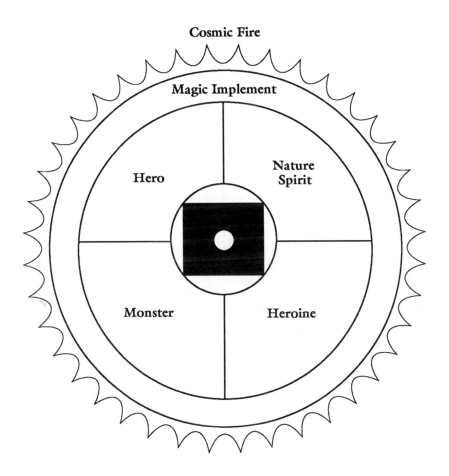

Androgyne Mandala

Results of the DREAM Process

Against the background of shifting paradigms which clarifies some basic ambiguities, and having discussed the alchemical processes which are the essence of all radical transformation, it is possible to describe some of the actual changes that take place in the participants, both as individuals and as performers, by virtue of the DREAM Process. Results may be immediate and dramatic as well as long-term and permanent.

It takes some years to see the full effect of the transformation process. In the case of both Charlotte and Tom, the transformation has been very favorable. Charlotte came to the work as a woman frustrated by a lifetime of robbing herself, through inhibition, of her chance to fulfill herself as a woman. She has become a happily married woman living an aesthetic life in Europe that she loves, while still pursuing her career. Tom came to the work drained of his power by acting out a dual life as a weak man and, compulsively, as a strong woman. He still dresses as a woman as part of his "outreach" work, but there is no longer the compulsion to do so nor the strains of a personality split.

To discuss results in general, several factors and variables need to be understood. Intense workshops, Rolfing and psychedelic sessions all have in common the value of wholeness. They also have in common that they are like "hits"—they may happen very deeply, but they also happen quickly. Unless there is some sustaining discipline to follow through and support the new way of being, the person slips back into old habitual patterns.

As magical as the process of transformation may be, the nitty gritty of actual change ultimately comes down to taking responsibility for monitoring oneself over time and bringing oneself around completely. A lot of people expect change to be done to them if they take a hit of LSD, or do a workshop, or have their bodies realigned. This is like having a bath and expecting to remain permanently clean. These media of sudden change seldom really work without a sustained and continued effort on the part of the person in transition. I have many friends who work in the helping professions, lead workshops and do body work. They all say the same thing: *ultimately, well-being and fulfillment of transformation is the responsibility of the individual.* For this reason, the first axiom of the Arica Work is, "You are responsible for your own evolution."

In addition to the commitment to take this responsibility for one's own continuous development, there has to be some way of sustaining the Work on oneself provided in the training itself. The most effective techniques and media of change therefore are those that train participants how to take responsibility to continue working on themselves by further exercises and practices. Here are some ways that the Work is continued in the ORIGINS Process.

In the course of the DREAM Stage there are very specific techniques passed to the group for dealing with the Monster and continuing with the development that is set in motion by the Process. These have been described in discussing the transmutation of the Monster. All of these techniques come down to the personal responsibility for monitoring one's own transformation. In a way it is like the discipline of the old paradigm, except that rather than attempting to shape oneself as an ideal, the discipline of remaining aware and surrendering oneself has the goal of allowing the unfolding of the whole.

In ORIGINS the continuation of the transformational work is built into the Process itself. After the individual work of the DREAM is completed, the group goes on to the MYTH and RITUAL which throws them into many situations that require them to apply what they have learned. These later Stages also involve the same Work at a collective level, so that each participant is having to process the archetype with the group and thereby continue the Work in another context.

The results of the DREAM Process for any person varies according to whether he continues in the further Stages, the degree to which he throws himself into the Process as it is taking place, and the way he continues to apply his new understanding using the techniques and processes that are presented. Given these provisos, some results can be discussed.

Actual Transformation

By actual transformation, I mean permanent change: someone who is definitely one way when he walks in and permanently another way when he leaves. I have seen countless transformations of this kind in the course of my work. Recently, in Germany, I worked with a professional actress who was unable to improvise on stage. During the Process she went through a crisis, stayed with it, and overcame her fear. She claims she will never again be inhibited about getting up on stage and performing extemporaneously.

People who permanently drop neurotic symptoms in these dramatic ways have one thing in common: they are willing to throw themselves totally into the exercises. The key to such sudden and total transformation is in the cathartic portions of the Process, specifically in the creation of the Monster and in the psychodramatic performances. There is a certain kernel of affect that is at the core of every Monster. There is also a specific gravity toward that kernel. If the person can abandon himself to the gravity until he reaches the kernel and explodes with it, the transformation actually takes place right there in the group. It is quite amazing and very real. There is no more beautiful theatrical moment than such an explosion. But only those participants who can reach a high level of trust and abandonment and are ripe for such a change will experience such dramatic results.

Awareness: Monitoring the Long-term Process

Almost everyone who completes the DREAM Process gains new awareness of himself by coming to see the real drama behind all the apparent dramas of life. Every participant also arrives at a new understanding of the Self and its development toward wholeness. This understanding yields an ability to monitor and interpret one's present development in terms of a greater context. The DREAM Process clarifies the context so that continuing growth can happen in a field of understanding that gives greater equanimity. In a sense, one could say simply that the Witness is strengthened. One does not get identified in the little dramas, because one sees them in the context of the greater drama—and from the perspective of the Witness.

I always tell the participants in my groups that when you bring one of the archetypes to bear in the Process, you have a kind of cross-section of the present Self. If you could imagine taking the Self here and now and doing a cross-section of it, you would have a kind of diagram of where you are right now in the grand process of your individuation. In a sense, the Dream is just such a cross-section. This section of the present Self gives a great deal of information about what is going to happen in the future. This is the in-depth life drama of your present. The future is also there; not future facts, but future issues, because the archetypes are the laws of change. Having a context within which to deal with and understand subsequent development is a healing predisposition toward crises that are yet to unfold. The future interpretation of these crises in terms of the symbols in the Dream helps the Hero to shape his continuing course. It is a kind of map by which to find one's way.

Meditation Exercises: Expanding Transformation

In the case of the Love Story, the two principles of activity and receptivity have to be worked in a continuing way. The action of the Love Story has to do with freeing up and clarifying the masculine and feminine possibilities in the Self and the experience of their pure balance. At the end of the DREAM Stage of the Love Story, several sessions are devoted to grounding the awareness that has happened through the symbolism of the archetype. The Work in these final sessions demonstrates the state of the androgyne, the experience of being purely balanced between activity and receptivity, so that this state can be recognized in the future and interpreted as the optimal condition to work toward.

The freeing and clarification of the active and receptive energies has happened largely in the work on the creation of the Hero and the Heroine. Clarifying these principles in depth requires supplementary work over a longer period of time, because the distortion of these principles by the Monster is very deeply habitual. The Monster that overlays the *yin* principle is the distortion of one's negative memory in the relationship to one's mother. Likewise, the negative memory of one's relationship to the father distorts the capacity to free and clarify the *yang* principle. This "negative karma" with the parent of the corresponding sex has to be cleared in depth.

To continue this work, the Neophytes are given a ritualized meditation, which I have adapted from an Arica exercise called "The Eyes of Karma." The meditation allows for a cathartic clearing of the "karma" with the parent of each sex and creates a space within for the clear energy of the *yin* and *yang* principles to manifest themselves. In brief, it allows the Neophyte to drop the charged memory, to open to the pure energy of the essential principles within, and finally to give each principle its balanced due. The Neophytes are instructed to do the exercise at least ten times. It works beautifully and powerfully and clears the way for further integration.

HOMEWORK

• *Needs*

> Androgyne Mandala completed
> Three white candles
> Two 3 x 5 white cards

• *Meditation (to be done ten times on ten different occasions, preferably*
> *at 11 p.m. before sleep)*

Salutation, RAMs in three centers

Mother (the feminine)
> Write mother's complete name on card
> Arrange card and candles as shown
> Maintain even breath
> For ten minutes, send a wave of love and wish her the highest
> possible spiritual evolution
> For five minutes, ask that the *yin* principle manifest in you to its
> fullest, feeling entire body black

Father (the masculine)
> Write father's complete name on card
> Arrange card and candles as shown
> Maintain even breath
> For ten minutes, send a wave of love and wish him the highest
> possible spiritual evolution
> For five minutes, ask that the *yang* principle manifest in you to its
> fullest, feeling entire body gold

Alchemical Union
> Sit in *yin-yang* mudra for five minutes
> Inhale gold from head down
> Exhale black from feet up

Androgyne Mandala
> Contemplate keeping even breath

Salutation

Contracts: Grounding the Transformation

In order to ground changes that have taken place in the Process, I often use Paul Rebillot's practice of having Neophytes make contracts with each other, duly signed and dated by the two parties.

At the end of the Hero's Journey, the group is put through a guided fantasy where they bring their Reward into various aspects of their lives and see how their "home" situations are altered by the Reward. This is the new *status quo*, and to actualize those changes each person makes concrete contracts with another group member. Here are some examples:

I, _____, promise to redecorate my apartment within six months. I will purchase the new furniture within three months and complete the remodeling by six months from this date.

Signed,

"_____" and "_____"

I, _____, promise to call my ex-wife and make a date with her. I will explain that I was mistaken in doing _____ and will ask her to forgive me and invite her to enter into a new kind of friendship with me in which we will _____, _____, _____.

Signed,

"_____" and "_____"

Partners are asked to communicate with each other periodically after the training in order to confirm that the contracts have been carried out. In this way, transformation is often very concretely grounded and definite changes in life are made permanent.

The DREAM and the Art of Performing

The DREAM stands on its own as an experience of universal value, benefiting anyone, be they performer on non-performer. But for the training of the performer, there are very special values to be had in the DREAM Stage, both as a holy performer and on the level of personal development in performing. This is the double value of the ORIGINS work: working on one's art is at the same time working on one's potential as a human being, personally and spiritually. The ORIGINS Work transforms the art of performing into a spiritual discipline of Self-realization.

As part of the feedback and analysis of the psychodramatic performances in the DREAM, evaluations are given on the basis of what we call the ORIGINS Code of Excellence. These standards include the following:

- Amount of let-go and abandonment.
- Visceral quality of the performance.
- Quality of resonance set up in the audience.
- Originality of the piece.
- What the performer allowed himself to do that he has never done before.

On one level, each of these criteria refers to the quality and quantity of let-go manifested in the performance of the Dream. These elements of performing and their importance in developing the skills necessary for entheotic performing have already been evaluated in discussing the benefits for performers in the CHAOS Stage.

But there is a second level of these criteria that has to do particularly with the Apollonian elements introduced in the DREAM, that vast ocean of universal form in personal manifestation. The performer is letting go *into* the archetypal forms that are the content of the Dream. He is letting go of his ego-controller *into* the Self-controller whose reservoir is the archetypes of Being, which, through the performer, have a life of their own. These are the channels through which the Dionysian energies of the Mothers are passing. They resonate in the common viscera which is the home of the Mothers. It is surrender to these forms and understanding their value and meaning in the process of human transformation as well as the access to the common viscera that constitutes the basic benefits of the DREAM for the performer *per se* and for enhancing the act of performing.

The characters in the Dream cannot be crafted as careful constructs created to fulfill some subtle character ideal; they come out of the Self and have to be portrayed with the totality of the Self. It is wholistic performing. In other words, this is not a careful construction of a mask, but the total expression of the sub-personality from the depths that makes the portrayal real in any case and sets up the appropriate resonance in the audience.

In fact, what one is doing is allowing the dynamic of the Mothers to express the super-personal form, the archetype. This, more than anything else, affects the originality and visceral quality of the piece. To the members of the group who are watching the performance, it is very clear just where, from how deep within, the performance is coming. Some of the perform-ances are expressing personal concerns and prototypes; others are dealing with universals. These variables are also discussed, because they are part of the dynamic that sets up resonance in the audience that is experiencing the psychodramas.

Through this work, one is learning to "channel" sub-personalities. One is learning how to engage the deeper reservoirs of the Self within. One is familiarizing oneself with the archetypes, the basic forms of human existence, the one human. This is also strengthening the possibility for setting up a deep resonance in the audience, the level of resonance necessary for sacred performance.

In this Stage, the performers begin to experience states of altered consciousness. When the archetypes begin to speak through the performer, when the Self is expressing itself in a truth beyond the control of the performer, there is a kind of lightness that happens. The truth coming forth is profound, visceral, moving—one has a blissful sense of *being performed*. We describe this as "flying," because that is the sensation one has. One ab-sents oneself and the inner performer takes over. These are the first fleeting experiences of the *satori* of entheotic performing.

The performer stands to benefit especially from the work on the Monster. For this reason, one of the most important features of the Work is dealing with the artistic ego, and one of the most powerful benefits of the entire Process is that one comes to understand how the transmutation of the ego-Monster is both part of the release of greater and greater performance power and the main spiritual work in Self-realization. It becomes very clear during the DREAM that dealing with the Monster is the *real* drama behind all the little dramas of life, especially the ones that performers tend to dramatize on a personal level.

The Monster is not only the biggest enemy of the performer, but also of the performance itself. In the MYTH Stage the personal Monster that has been seen and dealt with for the first time in the DREAM will raise its head in the context of the group project. It is advantageous that the performers have a chance to experience the Monster first in this individual context, so that they have no grounds later for feeling personally attacked. It becomes clear that the core of the Work is focused on one's personal Monster. It is by virtue of the DREAM that the ground rules and object of the game of co-creation are agreed upon by each Novice.

In the end the greatest value of the Process to the performer is that he understands the grand issues of human existence as they manifest in his own core life drama. Each Dream reveals how the stuff of all drama manifests existentially as the core drama unfolding here and now in one's own life. One is part of the ongoing Origins of all human life, of which one's here-now drama and the great dramas of culture—of all culture—are the same manifestation.

These benefits for the performer are part of both ORIGINS trainings. But each archetype and the training associated with it gives something special to the performer.

In the case of the Hero's Journey, the particular value to the performer is accessing deeper and deeper aspects of the Self. These deeper aspects come forth as the Hero's Journey progresses, specifically with the uncovering of the three aspects of the Monster. The refusal of the Call to Adventure corresponds to the fear of trying something new, the desire to remain in the same old performance habits. The confrontation with the inhibiting Monster is fighting to free the essence to express itself. And finally, the Supreme Ordeal gives the performer access to the deep internal primal energies which, until uncovered by the Hero, are working in a Self-destructive way. As the Hero goes deeper, energy is freed at a deeper level. The use of the Magic Implement also becomes more and more powerful as deeper levels of the personality are involved.

In the Love Story Training, the entire instruction into the nature of receptivity and its balance with action is vitally important. The training in receptivity is the precondition for opening to Being and to the depths of humanness. Likewise, the training in the nature of pure activity is vital because one comes to understand the pure act, without decoration or egoistic elaboration. Pure performing from the depths requires both—and both in pure balance.

This double ability and balance is particularly vital in entheotic performance. One must be purely receptive to the archetypal sub-personality within and to the other performers. There can be no competition. There can be no competitive ego. And one must be purely active to express what is received from the Mothers and to act when the situation is given to act. There can be no hesitation. There can be no reticent ego.

There is authentic mysticism to this. At the end of the Love Story, there is a session which progressively shows how active and receptive have to be constantly in a dance with each other. Each moment in life has its appropriate balance of activity and receptivity. As the balance between the two becomes more and more subtle, there comes a point when pure balance is reached. Here one touches into the mysticism that makes entheotic performing, in its pure form, ecstatic. It is one of the basic mystical aspects of the art of sacred performing; very real, very practicable, and inimitable.

At the end of the DREAM, each Neophyte has been sole producer of an entire production. Each of them knows how to do everything in the creation, preparation and performance of the production. Because each was the sole creator, each has seen what it is to function as a unit, a knowledge that will be needed when it comes time for the entire group to function in unity under pressure. The standard of unity has been set!

Transformation and Swami Anand Veereshwar

Having described the DREAM Stage and its results, it is appropriate to address my own role in this Stage of the Process. In doing so I call upon my own Witness and my understanding of this work as a transpersonal psychologist and scientist of the human developmental process.

As mentioned earlier, I feel that in the DREAM Stage the role I play corresponds to that of the shaman in a tribal situation. A shaman is a medicine man or a healer. He is a "magician" in the sense that he has an intuitive and working grasp of the powers behind power and the drama behind dramas. He heals members of the tribe by awakening them to other orders of reality. He provides the experience of ecstasy and he opens up the visionary realms, thus bringing forth from the depths the healing powers of the Mothers of Being. The healing that he performs may be physical or psychological. It doesn't make much difference, because in this work, healing of both kinds comes from the same source.

The shaman utilizes the imagination, the symbolic function to give form to a cosmos that is experienced as unpredictable. Even in the course of wild initiatory trances, the rendering of a chaotic psyche into symbolic form is essential. This process we have seen in the language emerging from the CHAOS Stage. Order is drawn from chaos; form is given to psychic confusion; the Hero finds the direction through a deep clarification of his journey.

The shaman also provides a diseased person or a malfunctioning group with a language by which unmanifested and otherwise inexpressible psychic states can be immediately expressed. It is the transition to this symbolic and performable expression that induces the release of the healing process by making it possible to undergo, in an ordered and intelligible form, a real experience that would otherwise be chaotic and inexpressible.

When I look deeper into my role in this Work, I am astonished to see how correctly its nature and function were originally characterized in the name given to me by Rajneesh when I became his disciple in 1975—"Swami Anand Veereshwar."

"Swami" is a title which was given by Rajneesh to all his male disciples. It may mean Master, teacher or just "boss."

"Veereshwar" is a name of Shiva. Shiva has many manifestations. Sometimes he is called the god of destruction, because he destroys ego—that which blocks the dynamic of change. He is actually the god of transformation. He is the Lord, the essence of the dynamic of transformation. We could say that he is the principle behind the two archetypal plot forms.

The word *veere* connotes "Tantric heroes." Tantric heroes, like those in the ORIGINS Process, surrender their egotistic inhibitions into their greatest fears and thereby come to wholeness. There are Shivaite sects in India that practice special forms of ritual surrender in these ways. As Tantric heroes, they worship the god Shiva who is their Lord.

In the *Shiva Puranas*, Shiva presides over eleven heroes whom he sends to the earth to destroy the Monsters that militate against the dynamic of transformation. In our terms, Shiva is the active principle of the Mothers of Being who sends forth the Magic Helpers and the Spirits of Nature. In this manifestation, Shiva is known as "Veereshwar." The name means "Lord of the Heroes" or "destroyers of ego."

This is precisely the function of this Process.

There is also the other name, "Anand," which means "bliss," or the state of *satori*. This to me names what I *experience* in this function. It is as though I disappear and something else is leading the Work. When I disappear in this way, I am in bliss.

So this is who I am in the Process—the bliss of the Lord of the Heroes. My "role" in the Process is *Anand Veereshwar*.

The DREAM is completed. The Neophytes have undergone an authentic transformation through the power of the archetype. The characters in the individual Dream and their source are clarified. The action is comprehended as the expression of the laws of transformation. This is not so much a "secret doctrine" as it is a mystery that the Neophytes now understand experientially and existentially. They know the power of the archetype. They understand the Self as constellated through the archetype. And they know how the Self gives expression to its flowering through the symbol system of the archetypal plot form. They have experienced the one Being that all human beings are— the One who encompasses the entire human cosmology and is Divine.

The Neophytes become Initiates. They now understand the mysterious Origins of Dream and are ready to give form to their Myth.

Summary: DREAM

The APOLLONIAN: Dream and Its Function
The Archetypal Plot Forms
    Archetypes
    The Plot Forms
The Dream Process
    The Evocation and Analysis of the Characters
        Movement and Stance
        Guided Fantasy
        Art Expression
        Presentation Performances
    The Action and Analysis of the Plot Form
Two Dreams and Their Analysis
    A Hero's Journey: The Archetype of Change
        Charlotte's Dream
            The Characters
            The Action
    A Love Story: The Archetype of the Union of Opposites
        Tom's Dream
            The Characters
            The Action
The Central Dynamic and the Naming of the Unnamed Gods

Stage III: Myth

The group creates a version of the archetypal plot form which expresses its common Self, its "Myth." The performers, now called Initiates, create a story line and a "script" composed of commonly agreed upon cues, basic actions and lines. Parts are taken according to the specific expressive talents and needs of each participant. The Myth is then performed improvisationally before an audience which may participate in some form or another.

Myth

Ever since I can remember I have had a special love for myth, a special sense of its significance. Even as a child I knew there was more to these wondrous stories than was apparent. I was taught that myth was an attempt to explain the "real" world by poor ignorant souls who existed before there was "real" (scientific) knowledge. In accordance with this prevailing understanding, it was appropriate to describe something that is unpopular and ignorant by saying, "Oh, that's just a myth," such as the "myth" of male supremacy. I went along with this explanation for a while, but there was something else my heart knew, even if the curiosity of my mind was supposedly put to rest.

Later I read Claude Lévi-Strauss, the French Structuralist, who gave a more satisfactory appraisal in describing myth as the way that primitives made their life experience more meaningful. Myth was like a kind of logic—a fundamental way of bringing form out of chaos.

But none of this ever did justice to my intuitions about the actual significance of myth. I always had the sense that something tremendously exciting and unknown was behind these fantastical stories that seemed to emanate from every culture. And whatever it was, I knew that the need for it was in no way superseded by civilization and modern science. On the contrary, I sensed that my own longing for myth was indicative of a great need in our time and that the absence of myth in our civilization was a key to its discontents.

In my own education, I kept searching until I was satisfied. But I didn't really begin to understand myth until I experienced the importance of my own dreams, through analysis. If dreams are the access to the hidden but true being of the individual, myth is the access to the true being of a culture. Myth is the artistic and cultural expression of the archetypes and their influence upon the lives of human communities.

The Function of Myth

Almost precisely as dream functions in the psychological health of the individual, so myth functions in the psychological health of the community. In other ages and cultures, myth sprang forth in the same spontaneous way that dreams appear in a human being. The myths outwardly expressed in common symbols the movement and development of the community's primal experience.

Much is to be said for the view of the Structuralists, who stress the integrative aspects of the language of myths as a spontaneous way that the psyche of the community organizes itself into meaningful form in times of stress. The psyche that is emotionally saturated organizes itself by means of mythological conceptions that form an explanatory system. This system gives significance and direction to the experience of the group, particularly its suffering. What seems to be irrational and chaotic is found to be ordered, though perhaps paradoxically. What is socially unacceptable becomes the stuff of sacred social drama. The extraordinary dangers that are encountered in the psycho-physiological adventures of the soothsayer, shaman or group medium become at first bearable and then ultimately heroic. This is another level of transmutation of the Monster. In this way, myth facilitates the psychological and sociological health of the community.

Going deeper, we can say that mythological symbols are the language of the spiritual life of a community. This is why early explanations of myth seemed to me so "primitive." It is not ignorance about objective reality that is found in myth; it is sophisticated interpretation of the whole Being. For instance, the realm of the unknown, or unconscious, where energies lurk that have not been assimilated into the known or conscious world, was expressed in medieval Europe as the forest with its dangerous wolf. In Polynesia, it was the ocean with its conger eel and sharks. Myth is a language of images expressing truths which have no nameable physical manifestation.

The Absence of Myth
and the Pathology of the Time of the Double-Not

Just as the absence of dream or the inability to relate to dream symbols tend to be pathological for the individual, so the absence of myth or the inability to relate to it tend to be pathological for our culture.

When a society changes, it loses its symbols and has to generate new ones to reflect its new situation. In modern society, the basic myths associated with Christendom have lost their credibility, but there has not yet been a conversion of the conditions of our lives into mythical symbols. This is what is meant by Friedrich Hoelderlin's lines, "It is the time of the gods that have fled and the gods that have not yet arrived."

The first reason that myth cannot be regenerated is because conditions are changing too rapidly. The natural process by which myth is created is organic and slow. Rapid change makes it difficult to convert conditions into myths. No sooner does a myth emerge than it is superseded by new conditions.

The second reason that we have lost myth is the *hubris* of objective scientific truth. Everything today is supposed to be explainable through the disciplines of science, economics and politics. Where is there room for mythology? Everything is specialized, cordoned off into segments of reality that are comprehended according to objective laws. We are not taught about spirit: we have no mental disposition for it.

These conditions bring about the highly pathological situation which Hoelderlin called "the time of the gods that have fled and the gods that have not yet arrived." There is no access to the primary healing faculty of the spirit, its symbolic function. We are cut off from our primal symbols and the healing organization of experience that they afford. Our experience of existence is therefore chaotic. There is no basic understanding of the meaning of existence. It is true anarchy of the soul.

The Higher Objectivity:
The Laws of the Divine Human Prototype

The existence of the objective sciences generates a kind of blindness about whatever their methods cannot approach. But there is another objectivity that is beyond that of the physical sciences. It is the objectivity of Being as opposed to beings. It is the objective science of all subjectivity. In the terms of Oscar Ichazo and the Arica Institute, it is the objectivity of the Divine human prototype.

We are all one human being. The structure of consciousness is the same for us all. This one consciousness that we are is not just another being, because it is at the essence of Being itself and is therefore essentially mysterious—Divine. This is not to say that it is not comprehensible, but rather that it is not comprehensible as an objective science of beings.

Mythology gives forth a language of the Mystery of Being. The "double" of myth—that to which myth gives expression—is the logos of Mystery. This logos, or "mythos," is the law of Being expressed by the archetypal plot forms. The law of change is expressed in the Hero's Journey. The law of the union of opposites is expressed in the Love Story.

The laws of the mythos expressed in the archetypes define the higher objectivity of human experience. They are the basic "system" that stands behind the gods that have fled and the gods that have not yet arrived. They form the necessary basis for any new mythology.

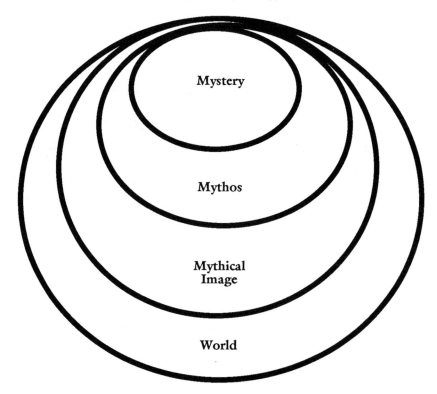

The Myth Process

The MYTH Stage of the ORIGINS Process consists in deriving and performing the Myth that expresses the collective Self of the group. The group continues working with the same archetype that was used in the DREAM Stage. In precisely the way that the DREAM revealed the Self of the Individual, the MYTH becomes the agent of group Self-awareness. The Myth is a medium for organizing the conscious and unconscious experience of the group in the context of its larger relationship to the world in general.

The purpose of the MYTH Stage is to express the central process of the group, its optimal development. It is a Process for common healing which is also effective at an individual level. The Myth expresses in its own way the process of each individual. In this sense it is a review of the DREAM, but in another sense it advances the case one step further by expressing the process of the common Self of the group. This creates a kind of vortex in which the individual process initiated in the DREAM is restimulated and activated in new ways, at other levels. People go through as many changes in the MYTH as they do in the DREAM.

If the myth is authentic, if it is a genuine evocation of the mythos, it goes beyond the truth of each individual. It also expresses the truth of the group, of the audience for whom it may be performed and, ultimately, even of the culture, the civilization and possibly the world. There has never been a "world" mythology, but I imagine that significant representatives from around the world in a group together could create such a mythology. This has been proven to me by the experience I have had working with international groups.

The challenge for the initiates in the MYTH is to penetrate into the true crisis of contemporary life and to name the unnameable gods. The group becomes a medium through which the conditions of the time express themselves in images, thus bringing into focus in a contemporary way the real spiritual problem of the community from which the group is drawn. This is the challenge, the fun and the wonder of the MYTH Stage.

The Creation of the Myth

The performers are now initiated into the mystery of transformation through the archetypal plot form that they worked in the DREAM. Each is still resonating from many insights and going through the manifold adjustments consequent to the experience of transformation in the DREAM. Each has the language and tools to deal with these changes, plus the presence of other group members when help or feedback is required. There is now a shift in focus from individual to group process, from the analysis of the individual Dreams to the task of creating a group Myth, staging it, and performing it before an audience.

The average amount of time that is taken for the MYTH is about two and a half days. Tremendous pressure is created by the short amount of time available. The pressure is part of the process. It throws everyone into a stressful situation in which Monster dramas and Magic Implements have to be used. It is a kind of crucible in which the multilevel teachings from the DREAM are put to the test and issues and matters unresolved heretofore show themselves in new guises.

The shift in focus from the individual to the group project means that everyone is thrown back up on the responsibility of dealing with themselves. All the tools for doing so have already been set out in the DREAM Stage. Each has to keep himself "clean;" there is no room for ego-Monsters. The creation of the Myth and the level of the group now become the focus.

The Group as One Psyche

As a natural result of the common experiences in the DREAM Process the group is gathering toward a remarkable coherence and unity. The feeling that "we are one person" is almost tangible, because there has been overwhelming evidence of it in the work. Each time the group sits in the circle to begin working and repeats the OM salutation and the RAMs, they are centering into this oneness. The ambience of the YES has also made everyone feel good about themselves, and when someone gets taken over by his Monster, the others quickly, and usually with love, bring him back into the group energy. This unity is such a dynamic part of the group by this time that I have to do very little in this regard. The group has become its own monitor.

The unity is necessary, because the group is now the entity that is coming under the power of the archetypal plot form, just as happened earlier for each individual in the group. It is the group that is now expressing itself through the archetype. Now we are going to create the Hero of the group, the Helper of the group, the Monster and the other characters. The group has to cohere into one psyche.

The unity is also essential in order to create the group Myth. Usually, at the outset, there is no story line and no script of any kind. This provides the "adverse situation" which the heroic group must overcome in order to create a production. The effectiveness is a function of enthusiasm and mutual co-operation. Therefore any divisive elements have to be assimilated or, in some rare cases, eliminated, and the group must be committed to making the "One Sound." In a sense, the One Sound is going to be the channel for the Myth.

There is tremendous excitement created by this "dangerous" situation. Here we are, about forty-eight hours away from a production to which friends and relatives have been invited, and we don't even know what we're going to do! How is this miracle going to unfold?!

Unless the participants are people with whom I have worked before, the group does not know that everything is under control. But I know.

Of the fifty or so groups that I have done, there was always some performance event at the end that seemed miraculous to everyone in the group. It just happens. It is an energy phenomenon that is brought about as a function of the group unity being channeled through the archetype and following certain very precise steps. I know the indices along the way; so do my assistant and those who have worked with me before. But for the Initiate, it is pretty hair raising. I know that in every group there will be at least two points in the Process where the whole thing looks absolutely hopeless (sometimes even to me). This is all part of the Process.

The main thing is that the unity of the circle contain within it a group spirit than can channel its true Myth.

Determining the Myth

From the outset, it is important to understand the difference between myth and allegory. An allegory is a story with a conscious underlying meaning whose elements represent political, spiritual or romantic situations. The characters in allegory usually stand for types of people or personifications of certain qualities. Jonathan Swift's *Gulliver's Travels* or Alexander Pope's *Rape of the Lock* are examples.

The difference between an allegory and a myth is subtle, but for ORIGINS it is very significant. It has to do with the way the story forms refer beyond themselves. The referent of the allegory is *conceptually or consciously* equivalent, so that what is said in an allegory can actually be said in another way, quite discursively. Allegory proceeds from intellectuals and philosophers. The referent of myth on the other hand is the mythos; its meaning is submerged. We are never quite sure, consciously, of what is meant. As in the case of the dream, the meanings of the myths are largely unconscious, mysterious. The characters and actions can be interpreted as a dream can be analyzed. There will be several levels of meaning. What is said in the myth cannot be said otherwise. Myth comes from its double, the mythos. It comes forth from holy men, shamans and mediums.

An allegory is a valid literary form in its own right, but from the point of view of myth, allegory is a kind of degeneration because it is no longer dealing with the unconscious, the mythos, the Mystery. From the point of view of the MYTH Stage, allegory does not reach deeply enough.

Until I understood this difference, I watched some of our productions err because they became too allegorical. There was a kind of flatness to them. They became like *Agitprop,* the theatrical performances dramatizing the socialist philosophy in the Soviet Union shortly after the Bolshevik Revolution. Now, while aware that the Myths do contain some allegorical elements, I am more careful to monitor these elements, subtly but continually, to prevent them from undermining the magic of the Mystery.

Creating the story line of the Myth is critical. The soil of the group is prepared by the work of the DREAM and by several other activities that happen early in the MYTH Stage.

At the end of the DREAM Stage, each member of the group is asked to think of two stories from diverse sources and to analyze the characters and the archetype in that story. For instance, the participants in a Love Story Training would be asked to recall a Love Story from a novel, a film, a play, a myth, a legend—any two of these sources. We spend one work session analyzing these stories. It is important to see the infinitely variable ways that the archetype actually works in the famous stories of the world. The Monster, for instance, may not be an actual character. In Jane Austen's *Pride and Prejudice,* the characteristics named in the title are the Monster, and they are part of the character make-up of the Hero and Heroine. By examining diverse stories, the group makes many discoveries that expand the possibilities for their Myth.

The process of creating the Myth is also prepared in the first session of the MYTH Stage, when the Initiates dance through the archetype. I narrate the story, the musicians play their improvisational accompaniment, and the remaining members of the group act out and dance the characters and the story, each playing all the different characters and sometimes playing off against each other. This "play through" usually lasts about forty-five minutes. Everyone has a wonderful time. They also review the archetype once again.

The way in which the story emerges from the group varies, but my purpose in each case is to find the deepest possible source. Sometimes the basic idea is already determined, as was the case in our first Love Story productions when we knew we were going to do our own version of the Hindu epic, the Ramayana. Sometimes the setting and costumes determine the story. (This is what happened, for instance, in the Spring Garden Ritual in Hollywood, described later in this chapter. The time of year, setting and costuming *were* images that adequately filled out the simple outline of the archetype.) Sometimes the group has a specific orientation. Once I did a training with only women participants. We knew that the story would be about a heroic woman and her struggle in the world. Sometimes the Dream of one of the members is particularly significant, and the group decides to use that as a story base. In one group there was an ex-policemen whose story of disillusionment with the police force became the base of the story. We called it "The Force." Sometimes there is a mediumistic personality in the group who has such a clear vision of the group Myth that his or her idea is accepted immediately. This was the case in Bali with the poet-philosopher Takdir Alisjahbana.

When none of these sources are present, I have the group split up into two or three subgroups. Each invents and stages its own story and presents it for the entire group in a small improvisation. Usually, one of these stories emerges as most appropriate. We did this in Amsterdam and two of the stories were so good that we created an elaborate Myth in which two love stories were intertwined, one between King Yang and Queen Yin and one between two human lovers.

Once, when everything else failed, a group with which I was working sat in a circle and meditated under the full moon. Slowly, as if in a trance, a story began to emerge, each person speaking when the spirit of the story moved them. It was beautiful.

In one of these ways, some basic story line emerges. A story committee chosen from the group meets during a break to set the story and work out its details so that the work on the enactment of the Myth can begin.

The Level of the Group

Second only to the creation of the story line, the level of the group has greatest importance in the MYTH Stage. The pressure of the situation has to be channeled in a certain way: Individual ego-Monsters, fired by this same pressure, have to be transmuted; the One Sound has to be tuned; and the group has to be cleared so that it becomes a channel for the healing power of the archetype. The performance is going to be an energy phenomenon. There will be a basic structure, but life will come into the structure through the improvisational and entheotic channeling of the group energy and its interaction with the audience. The group has to be high enough for the unnamed gods to descend.

The Monster in the Group

The Monster, who makes life in the Dream so interesting, is also preeminent in the MYTH. The basic principle is *to transmute resistance in the group into the characters and action of the play.* An attempt is made to find the fundamental characteristic of the ego and to portray it in the Myth as one character. Usually this main Monster will be surrounded by flunkies and assistants who emerge from the process of the group or have some relevance to the story. Thus the Monster is a kind of distillation of the individual Monsters in the group.

The most effective tool for identifying and dealing with the Monsters of the Initiates is an exercise called the *Line.* It is done in pairs, and everyone in the group is required to do it with everyone else at least once, and more times if there continues to be any difficulty between any two members.

The Line begins with a ritual. Two Initiates sit facing each other. They open and close the exercise with an OM salutation to their common essence. They repeat the RAMs in the three centers, and then each looks squarely into the left eye of the other. They repeat together nine times: "We are one person." This ritual centers them in the Witness and allows each to get in touch with whatever negativity may exist. The main exchange in the Line begins at the completion of this ritual. Each takes a turn of five minutes in which, without interruption, the active partner describes to the receptive partner any anger or other feeling that he has against the receptive partner, how his own Monster has created that charge and how the Monster of the other may have created it. Then the partners switch roles so the receptive partner becomes active, giving the same kind of feedback for five minutes. If there is no charged feeling, the partners exchange any other observations on the Monster of the other that may be helpful.

Not everything in a group is cleared up in this way, but a great deal is. Members of the group are asked to do the Line together on their own whenever there is any problem arising between any two of them. If the charge between them is very intense, another member of the group may sit by to strengthen the position of the Witness so that the exchange remains objective. In this way, Initiates have many opportunities to look at their individual Monsters in action on the scene, and charge between members of the group is clarified. Frequently, what transpires in the Line provides new action and characterization for one of the Monsters in the play.

It sometimes happens that an Initiate will become the focus of the Monster energy of the group and sabotage the group Process in some way. This matter is identified at once, and, if possible, incorporated into the play. One time a Heroine, out of frustrated love for the actor playing the Hero, struck herself down with a crippling back problem on the morning of the play. We rose to the occasion by changing the play so that the emphasis of the story was upon the incapacitation of the feminine principle, and the audience had to help her through her part. What this performance lacked in polish, it more than compensated for in relevant pathos.

The object is to maintain a close interface between the process of the individuals and the group as the Myth comes together. Process must continually be translated into image. All of this is part of the general transmutation of the Monster in the MYTH Stage.

The One Sound

The constant transmutation of the resistant elements in the group serves the basic unity. Each time the circle forms and the opening OMs and RAMs are done, there is greater emphasis placed upon the pure unison of the voices.

The demand for this increases with the need for greater group unity. Each individual sound must disappear into the One Sound.

Whereas individual work was the focus of the DREAM, all the work in the MYTH is interactive. Between the rehearsals there is support work in which the capacity of the group to interact and perform together is strengthened. There is dance improvisation and movement exercises done in pairs and with the entire group working as one organism. All of these contribute to the unity of the group.

Clearing the Entheotic Channel

The remainder of the support work is intended to increase the capacity of the Initiates to surrender to the group, to the archetype and to the energy of the production—to become a pure entheotic channel. There are cathartic exercises and let-go techniques, and exercises to clear the body, heart and mind centers and the expression that is emitted through these channels.

Particularly important is cultivating the body as the pure vehicle for physical expression and the heart as the channel for feeling. One of the most beautiful exercises is called Validation. The Initiates sit in a circle, and each takes a turn describing to the group the most objectively beautiful aspect of his neighbor's essence. As they become proficient at this, the validations become quite poetic, and the beauty of the group energy rises and rises until everyone is almost speechless. The energy of pure heart descends like an angel upon the group. This energy is carried into the performance and clears the heart for a real exchange with the audience.

The Enactment of the Myth

At the end of the MYTH Stage there is a production in which the group Myth is enacted improvisationally before a small audience, usually of invited guests. The Spring Garden Ritual in Hollywood described at the end of this chapter was the first of these performances. In the early Bodhisattva training, this performance of the Myth was the culmination of the Process. The transformation of the individuals and the group was completed and the performance was its flowering. The early performances were experimental in the extreme. They were a forum for whatever anybody wanted to try.

When the final stage of the RITUAL was added and the name of the organization was changed to ORIGINS, greater emphasis was given to the final performance as a work of art rather than the training as a Self-realization process. The production of the Myth then became a prototype for the Ritual which is the final product, a finished production. The audience of friends became part of the project in that their feedback was incorporated as a significant step in the process of creating the Ritual. They became an extended part of the group, and what they said caused us to alter, modify or significantly change the production.

Once the basic story is worked out, the process of creating the production continues in a very organic way with certain constants. Here are the essential elements.

The Score

There is no script as such either in the MYTH or in the RITUAL (though a full script has been written from one of our productions in Indonesia). Instead, we create a basic structure which I call a *score*. The score is actually a chronological list of agreements, made by the group, which constitutes the structure of the production. These agreements include basic and minimal actions, lines, blocking and musical notation. A score for an hour-long production might be about four typewritten pages, double-spaced. (See end of RITUAL for an example.)

The creation and mastery of this basic form has priority over all the other activities of the MYTH Stage. It is the skeleton of the production. It is like a vehicle that carries the energy of the group. When the group is grounded in the score, they can simply become carried away in it. They can improvise, they can enter into entheotic performance in any way they want as long as they keep returning to the score.

The production is half form and half pure, dangerous, vibrant entheotic performance. The grounding support of the score is vital, because when the level of the group is really high—and this is the purpose of the support-work—the gods come down to earth and play. The score makes entheotic performance possible.

The Source

Much of the score and most of the performance come from improvisational work of a very special kind. When an Initiate is assigned a character to play, he is asked to do certain kinds of meditations. The actual technique is

to translate awareness of inner qualities and sub-personalities into image,
action, character, and world. If someone is playing a Monster that blames,
I tell him to go inside and see how his own Monster convinces him internally
to shift blame onto something other than the real internal cause. This is a
special kind of technique requiring a very sharp awareness. The authenticity
of any characterization depends upon this awareness. In this way, too, each
of the performers has to sharpen the tools of spiritual development, his own
internal witness. It is amazing how difficult this is. As soon as you try it, you
see that the Monster is there at every step trying to obscure what is so.

To deepen this process of characterization we do an exercise in which
each Initiate gets up in from of the group as his character in the play. First
the character expresses itself in silent pantomime, then he describes who he
is, what he does in the play and why, and then he answers questions about
himself directed by the group. This allows the performer to fill out his
understanding of the character, its symbolic value and inner logic.

Another source of character and action is synchronicity. Many things
happen by accident in the rehearsals and, if one is very aware, such
"accidents" can be used to enrich the character. A flexibility has been
developed by this time and the performers become quite adept at using
whatever happens around them to strengthen their characterizations.

The amazing thing is that when one has a gracious attitude toward
happenstance, existence begins to cooperate by sending out synchronistic
offerings. You are not satisfied with your dialogue as the Nature Spirit, then
suddenly, as you find yourself speaking to a disconsolate member of the
group, just the right words "come along." New bits and actions are added
because of what comes up in the Line. Or someone wears an inappropriate
outfit that would be just perfect if we had a character to wear it—so we invent
one and the character turns out to be just what we needed.

During the MYTH and the formative parts of the production for the
RITUAL, anything that happens might get translated into part of the production. There is a general spirit of openness and a willingness to try anything.
This is a disposition from the People Theater of the sixties and early seventies
that works very well, even magically, as the production is being formed.

The Casting

Up until this point in the training, talent has not been a consideration. Expressive power and originality are far more important. To some extent technique and craft, often instruments of the Monster, have stood in the way of genuine performance. If the particular training ends with the MYTH Stage, these criteria hold. If, however, the training is oriented toward a major production, there is a shift in values in the Process whereby questions of talent and training become more predominant.

Even so, the casting is usually synchronistic and natural. Many of the characters are inspired by individual performances from the DREAM, and the Initiates have already well demonstrated their individual capacities in the many performances each has given. The process of casting is very organic, and everyone is somehow always perfectly cast. Some of the characters are cast according to an external appropriateness, because they obviously fit the role. Others are cast out of a gestalt appropriateness; that is, they play a part that fills out their totality by requiring that they amplify and play out some hidden part of themselves. For instance, Charlotte might be asked to play a leper, or a joyous and feminine Nature Spirit. Tom might be asked to play a very macho hero. Usually, Initiates cast in these parts play them amazingly well. A third possibility is that someone is given a part in which he needs to see himself in an exaggerated way. For instance, Charlotte might play a Monster who is very ascetic, or Tom might play a Monster that is a cynical and frivolous woman. This caricature feeds the Witness of the Initiate and augments the transformation process set in motion in the DREAM.

In these ways the casting of the Myth often furthers the awareness or empowerment of the Initiate. Knowing this, the performers bring a special zest to what they are doing, whereupon their individual transformation is enhanced.

The Directing

Due to the organic way in which the production comes together, the directing of the Myth is an art form in itself. I usually did the directing in the early productions, until I clarified for myself what the director's job actually is: a role with distinct duties and a definite procedure. Then I began turning the director's role over to others in the group. Now that the RITUAL Stage has been added and the production takes on another level of importance, I look for a director among the participants at the beginning or in advance. He or she is very important to the level of the performance.

In the creation of the Myth production, the director has to function as a channel for the directorial energy of the group. In the spirit of the Great YES, the Initiates are discouraged from making criticisms and negative comments about what does not work, but all positive suggestions are entertained. It often happens that one or several members of the group get "on a roll" and have lots of good ideas. The director has to be receptive to these suggestions. As the time-pressure builds this can be a very chaotic process for the group and often arduous for the director to field the suggestions.

This is inevitably a major learning experience for a director. He has to be receptive to ideas. In fact, he has to be a flexible directorial channel for the group. To this end, he has to balance his receptivity to the group's suggestions with his active authority as the group spokesperson. There comes a time, of course, when we get down to the wire and everyone simply has to allow the director to take over completely.

The director is responsible for the blocking, the score, the walk-through and ultimately the production.

The Music

The entire Process is greatly enhanced when there is music. In fact, it is almost essential, as it incites the Dionysian wave and thus greatly enhances and fulfills the entire Process, particularly all the catharsis, movement and dance.

Music is almost essential to the production as well. There have been some interesting performances without it, but my own preference is to have every kind of performing in the show, and music is always a precondition for this. More importantly, music always endows the symbolic imagery of the Myth with another level of significance. As Nietzsche said, music is itself capable of giving birth to myth.

Because of the value of music, a most important assistant to me is a good music director. His function is to coordinate the music and the musicians for the entire process and the production. There are a few outstanding musical directors with whom I have worked a number of times, and I have had the privilege of working with a few musicians who are geniuses. There have been some who assembled large orchestras (we had twenty-five pieces in Bali), there have been small bands, and there have been some music directors who did the entire production on their own with a synthesizer and a wide range of prerecorded music.

The music director and his assistants participate in the entire process and create the music for the production in a very organic way. During the DREAM, while the others are entering into their characters through movement and dance, the musicians are entering theirs by creating the musical themes that go with each character. They use the movement sessions in the DREAM to experiment and jam, playing with themes as they accompany the mini-productions of the DREAM. They learn to be in complete synchrony with each performer, providing for each whatever music or sound is required. In this way entheotic music is created.

By the time the MYTH begins, the musicians have worked out basic musical themes for the characters and for the basic action. The music for the performance is created out of these themes woven together in leitmotifs. The musicians are part of an organic whole and need to be just as adept at integrating and improvising as are the performers. It is deeply satisfying to create and perform music in this way.

The Repetitions

The daily schedule for the MYTH Stage is as follows: morning session, blocking and creation of the score; afternoon, group energy and support work; evening, walk-through, full dress run-through, then feedback. This is also the schedule followed in the RITUAL.

The score work and blocking is done in the morning because it is the most gruelling. The director blocks the basic action, incorporating whatever has been added from the work of the previous day. After this work, if necessary, a new score is typed and given to the group. Each morning the blocking and score are amended on the basis of the feedback from the night before.

At the end of the morning session, the group should be able to walk through the score. A walk-through is an accurate repetition of the score.

There is no energy of performance in it; it is just walking through the basic cues and action and saying the basic things that have to be said. This includes all musical cues. For a performance of an hour or an hour and a half, this walk-through usually takes about thirty minutes. It is usually done just before the run-through.

In the evening there is a complete performance, including whatever costumes are available. It is treated like a formal performance. Unless things completely fall apart, there are usually no interruptions. Lately, I have taken to walking onto the stage during the evening run-through and moving people around or otherwise correcting things when it seems necessary, but in such instances I am treated as invisible. I learned this from a wise and great Balinese dance teacher.

This uninterrupted run-through is very important. It sets up maximal conditions for energy to move the group. Stopping and starting causes the energy to fall. A run-through without interruption also forces people to improvise, even when they forget where they are in the score. On many occasions, new things happen that subsequently get entered into the score. Everything that has been rehearsed during the day is tried out in the context of the whole. And finally, everyone gets a chance to see where the production is on any given day. Some of the evening repetitions have low energy. They provide those moments when it looks like it's never going to come together. But I persevere as though this were the natural course—which it is.

The Performance

Before the performance begins, the group does a meditation that takes about twenty minutes. The purpose of this meditation is to remove all resistance to the pure energy. The meditation includes a guided fantasy which varies slightly depending on which of the two archetypes is being performed.

In the case of the Hero's Journey, for instance, there are the OM salutation and the RAMs. Each participant is asked to envision himself acting through his part in the score as though he were watching a film. Then he is asked to get in touch with any resistance to acting through this part. He is told to imagine all of this resistance in the form of his Monster rising up in front of him. Then he is asked to envision his own personal Magic Implement and to feel its power filling him as he takes three deep breaths. He is told to hold the Magic Implement up against the Monster and to watch the Monster disappear. The meditation closes with an OM salutation. (The Meditation for the Love Story is presented in its entirety in the RITUAL Section.) This meditation puts a summary end to neuroses and jitters. From there, without speaking further, the group goes directly into the performance.

By the time of the performance of the Myth, the group has become accustomed to simply getting up and performing the piece, no matter what. They are not prepared, however, for the miracle that happens when there is an audience present. In the first moments of the performance, there is a kind of click; everyone falls into a place of ecstatic poise. If they are really grounded in the score, they are able to soar. Usually all of the participants exceed themselves and whatever they thought they were capable of doing. The group gets incredibly high, and all the travail suddenly seems irrelevant.

It is truly a flowering, with the group giving off the perfume of its high level and pure energy and sharing the fruit of its transformation with the audience.

Of the thirty or so pieces that Bodhisattva Arts and ORIGINS have performed, there has been almost every imaginable permutation and experimentation. We have done performances which took place in different rooms of a house. We have performed Gothic Operettas in gibberish in warehouses. We have done wild ballets in cathedrals. We have performed in almost every kind of space—even a few theaters!

We have also experimented with many types of audience participation. We've had audiences shouting, throwing things and storming the stage. We have had audiences divide—half with the Monster and half with the Nature Spirit—and wage various kinds of battle with each other. Once we had the Hero's army shouting I WILL, and the Monster's side shouting YOU WON'T. We've had them do tugs of war. We've had them chant and hum and breathe in unison.

The purpose of all of this has been to develop techniques for involving the audience in such a way as to overcome the separation between audience and action. *My* purpose in all of this experimentation is to find ways to recreate the experience of the Ramayana that I had the first time I was in Bali, when suddenly what was being played "up there" was moving within me. All of this has been experimentation for real ritual theater. Some of it has worked and some of it has not. For me, it was always experimentation. It was almost always a spectacle. The group inevitably gets very high from the performance, feeling as though it had experienced a miracle.

The final step of the Process is feedback from the audience. In those instances when the Myth is the final performance of the Process, we usually begin by having each member of the group share what it was like to perform. Then we ask the audience to share what they feel was successful and what was not, and also to ask any questions that seem appropriate.

If the group is continuing on to the RITUAL Stage, we regard the MYTH production as a prototype, one that can be improved, altered or even abandoned altogether in favor of a new start. The feedback therefore has primarily to do with what works and what does not work, what should stay as it is, and what needs to be improved.

Following is a description of our first production:

A Myth In Hollywood
(From a review of Bodhisattva Arts, by Richard Lawrence)

"The spirit of Carl Jung came to life in Nichols Canyon on Sunday afternoon, March 15, 1981. Bodhisattva Arts, the brain-child of William Pennell Rock, staged its first performance on the grounds of the magnificent house and garden of artist Rick Herold. Surrounded by trees, flowers, a running brook and the paintings of the artist, the archetypes of the Hero, Heroine, Nature Spirit and Monster danced and sang their eternal drama.

"The techniques of Dr. Rock and the director Rick Herold are similar to the work of Brecht, Artaud and Grotowski. The assistants to the Hero and Monster, dressed in white and black respectively, served as a Collective Unconscious (in Rock's words). They guided the audience in a procession from one scene to another in the garden. When the audience first arrived, the Collective Unconscious posed in various areas of the estate and conversed with the audience. While the dissolution of barriers between actors and audience was close to the work of Brecht and Piscator, the primal nature of the production also brought it close to the sense of theater as ritual and catharsis of Artaud and Grotowski.

"The characters wore either primitive masks of bark or flower petals or had painted faces. The sense of stage design was excellent. The action began in the downstairs studio of the house. The characters spoke a language that was either well-known by all the actors or else fluent gibberish, but the action was quite clear. The Hero and Heroine meet. The Hero leaves, and then the Monster and his coterie enter. One of the Monsters tries to tempt the woman with oranges, rather like the serpent in the Garden seducing Eve with an apple. The Monster and his army abduct the Heroine and drag her down the steps to the brook running on one side of the garden. The Hero returns and finds the Heroine gone. A Nature Spirit appears by the brook to tell the Hero what has happened and offers to help him capture the Heroine. At another part of the garden in a cave is the Monster's lair where the Heroine is kept prisoner. The Nature Spirit drops down out of the trees to tell her that help is on the way. In a large clearing, the Hero and Nature Spirit fight the Monster with spears. The assistants to the Hero and Monster cheer on their respective masters. After the Hero wins, the Heroine is brought forth, and the actors and audience drink wine together in a kind of communion celebration on a deck to one side of the garden.

"The most striking performances were by Sonia Pasquali as the Heroine and Marc Girard as the Monster. Pasquali was dressed in white veils. Her limbs flowed like water across the studio floor in the first scene. Her performance in the role of the archetypal woman was credible throughout the production. Girard strutted and growled fiercely in a convincing portrayal of the Monster, the demon in all of us that is opposed to truth, goodness and creativity. He wore a magnificent headdress of weeds and red and black make-up that helped to express the violence and sexuality of the character.

"Fred Russo and Warren Lockwood played the Hero and the Nature Spirit. Russo was strong and dynamic in his part; Lockwood was noble as well as spiritual in the way that he carried himself. The rest of the cast showed a lot of energy in supporting the four main characters and interacting with the audience. The musical arrangements and guitar playing of Bryan Mann, with the assistance on flute and percussion of Mircea Irimie and the vocal improvisations of Sara Bezar, added immeasurably to the mythic quality of the event.

"The Bodhisattva actors are not professional, but the rawness and vitality of their largely improvisational performances are superior to the slickness of commercial theater. I'm sure the spirit of Dr. Jung was delighted to attend."

MYTH: William Pennell Rock as the Monster in the Cathedral.

MYTH: One of the Monster's henchmen in the Garden Ritual.

MYTH: A Nature Spirit in the Garden Ritual.

The MYTH and the Art of Performing

In the DREAM, the protagonist in the archetype was the individual. But in the MYTH, the group is the protagonist and it is the group that is going through a transformation which willy-nilly pulls each individual along in its wake.

Performers are well-known for their egos—outrageous and otherwise. Pride stalks the stage; prima donnas abound. Stage-grabbers vie for the biggest parts. The existence of these outrages is precisely what often makes the performing arts a kind of living hell. Artists' egos characterize the profane performer. However characteristic and deep-seated these egos are, they are basically no different from other egos when it comes down to their cause, their roots in the Mothers. The tools for transforming them are also the same: awareness, Self-love and careful use of the Magic Implement.

The MYTH and to some extent the rest of the Process is a great ego trap. This is a vital function of any mystical school. Many features of the Process are designed specifically to exaggerate Monsters—individual and collective—for the Witness to see in no uncertain terms. To begin with, the story is being created and taking shape during this Stage. Parts are growing and shrinking at an appalling rate. Someone is given the lead in the morning, then the plot of the story is changed and the part becomes very small. Almost everyone in the group gets the "opportunity" to go through these changes, and the Monsters fall into all the traps. The Initiates have to remain in the Witness. This is the crossing that separates those who are capable of being holy performers from those who are inveterate ego-trippers.

It has happened that we have lost a few "stars" at this point, but there is always a great teaching for everyone. One thing is certain: A profane performer cannot be a real holy performer nor can he do entheotic performing. The whole valence of being on stage is an entirely different matter for the holy and the profane performer.

The individual performer goes through a great deal in this process. It is not a matter of just jockeying for the right part. It is all the work with Monsters in general, the ego resistance to clearing the channels, and working towards the One Sound. All of these provide splendid opportunities to meet and confront the Monster with the assistance of myself and of the supportive group and the techniques and exercises. And every transformed Monster means greater performing power.

MYTH: A circus Myth in Vancouver, Canada.

The group Process follows along with the object of the MYTH: to name the gods and to create a mythical expression of the group transformation. To this end, the essence of the group must express itself, and roles are given according to the needs and requirements of the Myth in process. There is a splendid opportunity for all kinds of play and improvisation. Give-and-take is everywhere required. There is also lots of practice in using whatever happens creatively. Some of the most appropriate elements of the characters, the story, and the actual production come out of these accidents and the playful attitude that is encouraged around them.

Perhaps the most valuable training of all is the act of creating the characters. What is required is a real and deeply enriching awareness process. It requires a demanding Witness of one's own inner workings, an ability to distinguish what is authentic and really works from what is unauthentic and dysfunctional. This happens through the technique of creating image, action and character out of the radical awareness of inner qualities, happenings and sub-personalities. This is a basic skill involved in entheotic performing. Gods are the archetypes manifest in us.

The spiritual transport felt by the Initiates in the performance of the Myth is the first real experience of entheotic performance—the ecstatic place of pure surrender to the mysterious energy of the archetypal plot form. At this point they realize that there is truly a divine force that moves through the archetype and propels them through its unfolding. It is a mystical state. Once they have experienced this entheotic disappearance into ecstasy, they are no longer Initiates. They are now ready to cultivate this state and to carry it to the people. They are ready for the RITUAL, and they are ready to become Priests.

The archetype is the divine law expressing the Mystery of Being. Myth is the natural way of expressing ourselves from the Mystery within, through the mythos, out into the world. The true, inner significance of myth has been lost to our object-oriented, de-mythologized consciousness.

I do not know if this is the proper form for creating and expressing our mythos, but when we find it a new order of performing art will come into being. So deeply has myth been suppressed, and so great is the hunger for its true inner richness, that when the significance of the truth of myth becomes manifest its content will explode upon the culture.

Summary: MYTH

Myth
    The Function of Myth
    The Absence of Myth and the Pathology of the Time of the Double-Not
    The Higher Objectivity: The Laws of the Divine Human Prototype
The MYTH Process
    The Creation of the Myth
    The Group as One Psyche
    Determining the Myth
    The Level of the Group
    The Monster in the Group
    The One Sound
    Clearing the Entheotic Channel
The Enactment of the Myth
    The Score
    The Source
    The Casting
    The Directing
    The Music
    The Repetitions
    The Performance
A Myth in Hollywood
The MYTH and the Art of Performing

Stage IV: Ritual

The performance of the Myth, modified by the feedback from the audience, is used as the prototype for a complete script which is mounted into a full-scale production. It is performed as an offering to five essentials: the highest development of consciousness, the archetypal plot form, the Spirits of Nature, the power of the Monster, and all of humanity.

An Experiment in Bali*

In February 1983, I came to Bali with a small group of artists from Bodhisattva Arts, Los Angeles. All of us were enchanted with this paradise and its volcanoes, deep green jungles, rice terraces, rushing waterfalls and sparkling beaches. Here we found a people and a culture that seem very close indeed to what nature had in mind for mankind.

In Bali the roots of performing art are still thriving as part of the value structure by which the culture perpetuates itself. Moreover, all the stages in the development of theater art are present and alive from the first beginnings in the expression of fundamental religious reality to the final degeneration into mere aesthetic entertainment.

Six years before, on my first trip to Bali, this enchanted land had provided me with new inspirations for giving shape to original artistic impulses. In particular, I found there a highly refined ritual-drama that transforms its audience by lifting it to a new level of Self-awareness. Since the time of these first inspirations, I had been seeking to recreate in the West a contemporary ritual drama form.

Our expedition to Bali in 1983 had two purposes: first, to study the practices of traditional ritual-drama; second, to gather together an international group of performers to create a contemporary ritual-drama. We had heard of the Art Center in Toya Bungkah, so after a few weeks in Bali we made our way up to the rim of the great caldera containing the volcano Batur, down its precipitous interior and thence, by canoe, across the crater lake also called Batur. Arriving in Toya Bungkah at sunset, we had the good fortune to connect immediately with Professor Sutan Takdir Alisjahbana. The con-

* From Newsletter, Summer 1983, International Association of Art and the Future, Toya Bungkah, Bali, Indonesia.

nection was intense, profound and inspiring. It was almost as though he were waiting for us. When I made known to the Professor our intention to create a new ritual-drama, he responded by offering all of his facilities, his artists and, perhaps most valuable of all, his visionary inspiration as an integral part of the group. The collaboration and the experiment began.

The group that gathered at Toya Bungkah was composed of dancers, actors and musicians. About half of them were Westerners, the other half Balinese and Javanese. The experiment took on new dimensions and difficulties because of the international nature of the group, their differing cosmologies and belief systems, and the fact that the work was conducted in two languages.

Some of the performers were experienced only in acting or in dance, with varying degrees of actual performing experience. A trio of particularly gifted Javanese performers connected with the Center were highly experienced in their own traditional movement forms, but also, surprisingly for me, extremely adept at improvisation and spontaneous performance. This ability is vital, since the entire production arises out of the inspired improvisation of its participants.

In the beginning, it seemed that the diversity of approaches to perform-ance and differing cultural backgrounds would never allow the requisite group coherence to evolve. But over the five-week period, dysfunctional elements were either eliminated or assimilated by the group Process. By the end, the miraculous melding of these manifold diversities into one coherent force became itself an inspiration, embodying the central idea of the ritual-dance presentation—that all human beings are one.

The ritual theater form requires various media for altering the con-sciousness of the audience. In this we were tremendously fortunate to have at our disposal the large gamalan orchestra of the Center. The gamalan is a complex musical medium, composed basically of gongs of greatly varying size, that is rooted in the earthy religious tradition of Java and Bali. Its sounds, at once primitive and refined, seem to resonate along the sensitive length of the spine and bring consciousness into a trance-like receptivity. In my first visit to Toya Bungkah, I discovered that the orchestra—consisting upwards of twenty-five players—was capable of improvising according to instructions or by following my improvised movement. This orchestra provided a medium which was invaluable for bringing about the states of consciousness necessary for training the performers. The gamalan also provided a significant consciousness-altering medium for the production.

The experiment, based on the archetypal plot form of the Hero's Journey, followed the stages established in the Bodhisattva Arts Process: CHAOS, DREAM, MYTH and RITUAL.

In the powerful cathartic exercises that initiated the Stage of CHAOS, the orchestra quickly brought the energy of the group to the requisite depth of cathartic power. Indeed, so powerful was it that a significant number of Balinese performers hurried out of the hall. In the absence of a priest who traditionally cares for them on such occasions, they feared that the music would send them into a trance from which they could not return. In the end, however, everything was quite in order, and no one who remained entered into any state from which there was no return.

The participants were brought to a place where, through let-go, each could perform a "ditty," a small improvisational piece, wholly spontaneous, without design, but having a compositional value ordered by the instinctive dynamic of the whole Self. To my surprise, as the animator directing a process devised essentially in the West, it was the Javanese who were most adept at this difficult marriage of elegant craft and instinctual expression.

The physical portions of the Process were at a premium because they required little translation or explanation. They were also particularly forceful due to the vital power of the gamalan accompaniment. As with all of our sessions at the Center, we were attended by local villagers and children who watched the goings-on through the windows and stimulated the performers to ever greater heights of expression.

Depending largely on the medium of movement, the participants created their Heroes and performed them before the group. There was a knight, a bird, an atavistic queen and others, each boasting of himself and relating the events experienced in the fantasy or expressing it through dance.

The evocation of the Magic Helper was held on a grassy slope between the lake and the cone of the great volcano. The Magic Helper was evoked for each participant by some item found in nature and brought into the tribal circle of the group. A flower became the power to transform each situation with love, a leaf became the power to see growth in all things, a stone became the power to still the mind with the awareness of eternity. Each participant then performed a dance portraying his spirit appearing to the group and bestowing the Magic Implement and its power. There was a tree spirit, a frog, the spirit of the lake, even the volcano—all performed to the sounds of flutes and drums.

That evening was the night of the Monster. Curtains were drawn in the performing hall and all visitors were excluded. Then, with the help of the gong orchestra, all ego-resistance—psychological inhibition and physical tension—was exorcised in the form of hideous Monsters. The curtains were opened and the villagers were treated to the physical manifestations of these self-revealed demons—in full, improvised costumes—doing their wild dances and submitting to the penetrating questions of the group.

With this, the three elements of change—the Hero initiator, the Monster inhibitor, and the essential Helper—were established. Each participant was shown how to see himself and his way in life as a function of these characters and their interaction.

The instruction was then given for each participant to create a theatrical production, playing all three characters and dramatizing how the Hero sets out from his home, meets the Helper who gives the Magic Implement, and confronts the resistance Monster, using the Implement to overcome the beast.

The group was given the next day off for preparation. Some of the participants made a heroic journey to the precipitous edges of the volcano to peer down into its steaming fissures. Others spent the day preparing for their performances. In the evening, on the torchlit stage, each played out his own inner drama, the drama behind all dramas. Some of the performances were spoken and acted, others were danced. Some were very short and terse; others, very long and elaborate. The villagers stayed on to watch late into the night.

The dramas that were being portrayed in the workshop stimulated many Hero's Journeys of a personal nature in the lives of the participants and, as factions coflicted, even in the progress of the workshop itself. Thus Monsters raged and sabotaged the proceedings, and Magic Helpers saved the day.

Only those who had successfully completed the "Battle" and could speak English were able to participate in the portion of the DREAM called the Supreme Ordeal. These brave souls experienced—through guided fantasy— the worst possible thing they could imagine. Each used the imagery therein to psychodramatize the basic fear that underlies the power of their own

Monster of resistance, which must be confronted and dealt with by the hapless Hero. Deep analyses were made of these Supreme Ordeals, so that the energy suppressed under this fear could be freed to empower the total person and the total performer.

Those who could pass through this ordeal found, in another guided fantasy, a symbolic reward of greater insight and power that comes from an authentic confrontation with the primal elements of existence and Being. With this reward, the Heroes returned to transform their homes to a new *status quo*...and, possibly, a new beginning of another journey.

For those who completed the DREAM, drastic changes had taken place. Each person was brought to a deep understanding of the process of transformation and its tangible manifestations. The Neophytes who completed the DREAM now had a working understanding of how the primal plot form expresses the Self and its growth. The archetypal characters were existentially understood, and the source of any character to be created in the Myth was tapped by one and all. The most important development was that everyone in the group understood how it is that all human beings are one— the One who encompasses the entire human cosmology and is Divine.

In the second session the group convened once again at Toya Bungkah for the MYTH. By this time the group energy was gathering steadily toward a real coherence.

The Center itself was buzzing with activity. At the end of this four-day period the Professor was to host at the Center a conference of poets from all the Southeast Asian countries. The dances that had previously been created by the Center were to be exhibited and had to be rehearsed. Moreover, it was determined that our group would perform our work in progress for the poets. The atmosphere at the Center was very charged.

The way in which the Myth arose from the group was determined by our circumstances of mutual interest with the Center and the Professor. We were a very international group convened at the Toya Bungkah Center and dedicated to considering the role of the artist as a visionary of the future. Moreover, since Professor Alisjahbana was working closely with us, it was inevitable that the Myth would reflect his vision. In time it became clear that the visionary artist and the Bodhisattva artist were one and the same. Our common cause determined our Hero and our Myth.

The Indonesian artists who had remained at the Center during the ten-day break between the DREAM and the MYTH had been asked to prepare one improvisational piece on the Hero's meeting with the Helper and battle with the Monster, with each performer taking a different role. On the first evening the Professor and I, together with the members who had dispersed during the break, were treated to this performance created and performed by three Javanese dancers. The subject matter was the emergence of a new kind of artist—his rite of passage. The dance was so exquisitely composed and performed and spoke so deeply to all of us present that is was clear the core of the Myth was already given. The remaining work was clear: to set the context of the story and to fill it out with the other performers in complementary roles.

Taking this core as our beginning, several members of the group worked together with the Professor and myself, and the story took shape with a velocity amazing to all of us. Its relevance for each participant was vital.

We followed the same schedule of work during all four days of the MYTH. Each morning we worked on the score. In the afternoons we did group exercises in movement or improvisation, the Line to clear emotional charge between members of the group by showing how particular Monsters were at war, or exercises to validate the essential gifts and beauty of each participant. These sessions functioned to raise the level of the group energy.

Each evening we performed the entire piece, such as it was, complete with full orchestra. With each performance, the ensemble came to a deeper unity, difficulties were worked out, and the story and production took definite shape.

On the Sunday night before the arrival of the poets, we performed our Myth. We had hoped the show would be sufficiently prepared to perform for the poets, but we were not quite ready as an ensemble. The program presented for the poets on Monday evening included the performances prepared previously by the Center and the small ensemble of three principal characters (danced by the three Javanese) performing the essential plot of the Myth, as they had the first evening. The power and vitality of their performance was stunning.

Though the group as a whole was somewhat disappointed that not everyone was able to perform, the situation wakened them to the level of performance required. It spurred them on to work harder and with even greater focus in the final segment of the Process.

Very conscientiously we took stock of all the audience feedback after each performance, particularly the detailed comments of Professor Alisjahbana, so that during the break of some ten days we were able to bring the score to its final, workable form in preparation for the fourth Stage, the RITUAL.

Prior to our trip to Bali, the fist three Stages of the Bodhisattva Arts Process had been developed through many diverse workshop experiences. The Stages of CHAOS and DREAM were perfected as forms of transpersonal therapy which proved very effective in releasing creativity and power and greatly enhancing self-awareness. The MYTH was added subsequently as a means of furthering the therapeutic process through the application of the acquired skills and insights to the creation of the theatrical piece or video drama which could spread the message of the group and the process to a wider public in an entertaining experimental form.

The purpose of our trip to Bali was to study authentic ritual drama in order to understand its objective form—that is, independent of its traditional context. Our method was to abstract out the objective principles of ritual drama in order to create efficacious entertainment that can have an integrative function for its public similar to that of ritual for its adherents. The goal, briefly stated, is *to create a contemporary performing art form that brings about transformation in the audience by carrying it through the archetype and projecting an integrative vision for a viable human future.* This goal fortuitously brought us to the Center, and, as the experiment progressed, it continued to deepen our personal and spiritual relationship with its visionary mentor, Professor Alisjahbana.

In the month before coming to the Center I had the opportunity to witness ritual drama productions throughout Bali in their native temple settings and to observe carefully the techniques by which drama is brought home to the sources of the psyche from which it springs. I found many clues for returning drama to its primordial efficacy as an instrument for raising consciousness and bringing about transformation. I also had the good fortune to meet many Balinese artists and holy men of the Brahmin caste who were able to articulate some of the principles I was seeking to understand.

During the break we had been able virtually to finalize the score. As the

Center was free during the RITUAL, the Professor and I, as well as the other resident members, were able to focus on the task of bringing the Ritual to its final form.

The piece was entitled EMERGENCE. A synopsis of the final story: The Mother of Love does an offering dance in the traditional form. With a loud NO to her, the Greed for Power enters. He calls forth his victims. Each one he corrupts, finishing his work by placing a mask over his minion's face. The holy man he corrupts into a fanatical bigot, the politician into a dictator, the businessman into an exploiter and the scientist into an irresponsible madman.

The artist Hero enters the world dominated by these four as the Monster looks on with glee. The artist tries to follow their dictates and even helps the scientist to discover the Great Bomb. The dictator grabs the Bomb and holds it precariously over the poor Hero's head. In a panic he runs from one to another of his mentors trying to find solace and solution, but instead he finds only confusion. In despair, he turns his back on the lot, leaving them to fight over the Bomb.

Despondent, the Hero sets out alone and, at his lowest point, is visited by the Magic Helper, the Mother of Love. She revives him and brings forth the Spirit of Air and Water who shows him that all men are the expression of God. To empower him with this vision, she gives him a shell. The Spirit of Earth and Fire brings him a flower, empowering him with the realization that man comes from nature and is responsible for nature.

With these powerful insights, the Hero returns to the world of the dangerous buffoons, gradually fending off their domination with his Magic Implements. The powers reduce the Monsters to baser and more reactionary exertions of power, but the Hero overcomes their influence upon him because he knows the truth.

The Mother of Love enters and gives the artist to realize that this is no victory, but rather the ordeal whereby he must come to terms with his own deepest egotism. She reminds him of the power of his Magic Implements and empowers him to do final battle with his own power greed. After a wild battle, the Hero destroys the Monster but realizes he has lost his own vital energy. Together with the Mother of Love he revives the beast who, now

RITUAL: The offering in Bali.

transmuted through the wisdom and awareness of the artist, serves him in his essential power.

Now the artist is a Bodhisattva. He has arrived at real spiritual integration. He has returned to original oneness. Love reigns above, the vital energies below serve his heart and he is able to look upon everything with loving power. Before this iconic paragon, the monster minions enter enraged. But the Spirits come forth, unmasking the Monsters one by one. The Spirit of Earth and Fire transforms the repentant businessman and the scientist by showing that they can reap greater rewards by surrendering intelligently to her ways—not to exploit, but to complement her so that she may nourish them in return. The Spirit of Air and Water appears to the dictator and the fanatic to show them the truth of God in every man. They repent and dedicate themselves to authentic service to mankind as its guide and shepherd. The Bomb is defused and its power deployed to the service of one humanity and one planet.

The Javanese dancers took the three primary roles. The two Spirits were played by two gifted and beautiful dancers from the West. The four Monsters were played as clowns by Western actors who spoke their parts in English. The Javanese spoke Indonesian and sometimes colloquial Javanese. The use of several languages permitted everyone in the audience to understand at least half of what was said and to intuit the rest from the action. Performing in several languages was also very powerful theatrically. In moments of strife, it exaggerated the essential misunderstanding between divided human beings. In moments of harmony, it demonstrated that the human heart in its understanding is greater than all human differences.

Many theatrical devices enhancing the immediacy of the message were borrowed from traditional Balinese drama, including the gamalan orchestra which cast its inevitable spell.

It was quite amazing that a full production was conceived, created and mounted at Toya Bungkah with only twelve days of work. The experiment was a great spiritual joy to all concerned, and everyone who participated was astonished at the effectiveness and vital power of the piece.

RITUAL: The slaves of the Monster fight over the artist Hero in EMERGENCE II

RITUAL: William Pennell Rock and the three great Javanese dancers in EMERGENCE I.

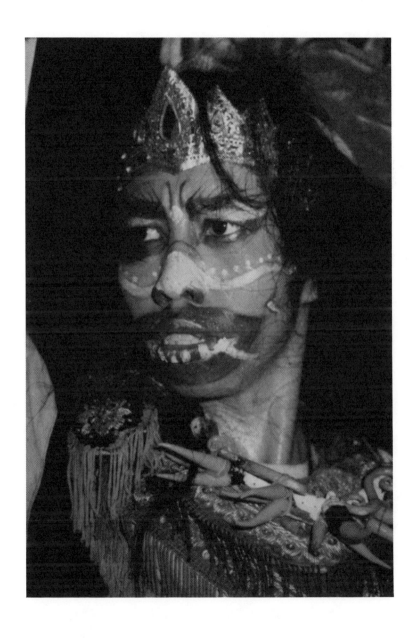

RITUAL: The Greed for Power in EMERGENCE II.

RITUAL: William Pennell Rock, Takdir Alisjahbana, the Mother of Love, the Artist and the Greed for Power in EMERGENCE II.

RITUAL: The Sacred in Action

The performer and the holy man who live within me have driven me on a search for the Source like a nomad over a vast desert terrain. This quest took me to the soil and roots of performing art—through psychology to the Self and the mythos, through philosophy to the most primordial ground of Being, through religion into the enquiry into the basic relationship to existence itself. Here, in religion, I found the well-spring, the ancient metaphors of the Sacred. Becoming a spiritual archaeologist, I began to discover the realities behind these metaphors—ancient footprints of the gods that have fled.

Now we come to ritual. Ritual is the medium of ceremony or performance through which the Sacred is brought to the people. Whereas myth is the image through which the sacred mystery expresses itself, ritual is the *presentational action* through which the Sacred expresses itself. But unlike myth, ritual is interactive. The Sacred gives; the man receives. The man gives; the Sacred receives. Back and forth, active and receptive, give and take. Authentic ritual is the interaction of the Sacred and man in *yin/yang* balance. This balanced exchange is the mystical essence of Sacred Performance.

Ritual has no more life than the Sacred that animates it. Like the mystical images which are empty if collapsed, ritual is empty if the gods are not truly in the temple of the hearts of the people. In a living religious tradition such as that of pre-classical Greece or modern-day Bali, the ritual is where the life, power and vitality of the gods is infused into that of the people. Ritual is a place where the Mothers meet and commune with the worshippers. The form of the ritual is the meeting place of the Sacred and the profane.

In its earliest manifestation, performance was ritual. The tragedies of ancient Greece are a development from earlier ritual forms of which there is no record. They were expressions of the cults of the primal Mothers of Being that worshipped the Mothers' son, Dionysus. Just as the archetypal Mothers reach through the Spirits of Nature to the Hero back through the initiation, so they reached through the performance ritual of the Dionysian cults to bring the community back to their Origins. The cult rituals of Dionysus were an initiation, a healing communion—reunion with the Mothers of Being. Only later, when the worship of Apollo became ascendant, did tragedy as such evolve into a great reckoning between the form of Apollo and the energy of Dionysus.

In India, too, the performing arts have grown out of the worship of the great gods and have been refined as disciplined forms of communion. Even now in India the archaic religions and their expression can be seen through the manifold and highly evolved performing tradition of the sub-continent.

In Bali, where the source of performance in ritual is still intact and alive, it is possible to glimpse what ancient Greek theater was like and to see the roots of theater still living in the soil of a vivid religious tradition. Performance in Bali is so vital and evocative, yet so sophisticated and accessible, that it is possible to have a truly primordial experience of the art, as I did during my first visit when I saw the Ramayana performed before the gates of the temple.

Ritual is an authentic access to the Mystery, the regenerative source of Being. It represents the most ancient, religious act by which man—always aspiring to transcend himself—reaches back to his Origins, regenerates himself and grounds himself in the Being that he authentically is.

The RITUAL Process

The purpose of the RITUAL Stage is to perfect a performance medium which brings the unnameable gods to the fore, to present to the public its relationship to these gods—here and now—and to offer this entire endeavor to the sanctity of the unnameable gods.

In the time of the double-not, it seems highly inappropriate to set forth a religion. The RITUAL Process amounts to the creation of a disposable or, as I sometimes call it, "cardboard" religion. The real Sacred element in the Process is the archetype behind the Myth and its transformative power. This sacred power is the unnamed gods.

Through the Myth, these unnamed gods become tentatively identified. During the Ritual these identities become icons of a mini-religion. The specific Hero, Heroine, Monster and Nature Spirits are actual icons of the archetypal energies, icons that the group has created out of their collective psyche. The Myth becomes the medium through which give-and-take with the unnamed gods can take place through the icons. The Ritual is the procedure through which the give-and-take happens.

The surface focus is the iconographic guises of the archetypes, but the real object of "worship" is the unnamed principles behind these icons and the potential wholeness which stands behind the archetype itself.

When the Process is completed, the icons are in a sense destroyed, but the powers, the gods behind, remain. Accordingly, the Myth and the Ritual production are said to be "cardboard"—their essence is true religion, but their form is disposable. This I feel to be the most appropriate response to the need of the time of the double-not.

A basic change in the Process takes place with the RITUAL Stage. It comes down to the difference between the group as a form of spiritual discipline or therapy and the group as a way of generating a work of art. In the first instance, the MYTH Stage suffices, culminating as it does with a performance for friends and family.

When the object is to create a finished production, the criteria and the dynamic of the group changes radically. There is a new imperative—-artistic quality. The talent and craft of the performers becomes relevant for the first time in the Process. This ups the ante on the entire Process. Old, profane performer Monsters rear their heads with renewed vigor and new tension is added to the group process.

Practically speaking, the RITUAL Stage consists in preparing a finished production based on the group Myth and continuing the support work to further raise the level of the group so that the production becomes an authentic Ritual. The daily schedule is basically the same as in the MYTH: blocking and script rehearsal in the morning; support work in the afternoon; and full run-through in the evening, followed by feedback.

At this Stage, my role becomes similar to that of the High Priest in the ancient performing traditions. I maintain the level of the group and I monitor the iconography of the emerging production—that is, I make sure that the characters, the dialogue, the action and the setting all develop and remain authentic expressions of the mythos and the Mystery. I lead all of the meditations and much of the support work, and sometimes I make an introduction, much as the Priest does for the ritual theater productions in Bali.

My preference is for all other functions to be delegated to the group. The most important, as I have already discussed, is the direction of the production and the musical direction. Over the last few years, I have been able to bring into the Process strong artists who have collaborated with me and contributed significantly to the productions. In the CHAOS and DREAM Stages, they do the work along with the group as much as possible, but by the time of the MYTH Stage their role becomes more and more important. In the

RITUAL Stage, I return to my priestly functions and the production is taken over by the director and the group.

At this point in the preparation, directing is not substantially different from the direction of a standard production, except that the director has been integral to the generation of the score and participates in all the work of the group.

I work extremely well with strong collaborators. I have never had a moment of dispute with any of them. I respect their talents, and my attitude to what they bring forth is basically YES. I always reserve the right to use the High Priest's veto, but almost never have to do so. It has only been invoked on the rare occasions when there has been a dispute over some production detail or another. I honor the complementary abilities of those with whom I collaborate, and I am grateful to them for the balance and substance they provide in this stage of the Process.

The script is created from the performance at the conclusion of the MYTH, which we call the prototype. The feedback from the audience is duly taken into account, and alterations—basic or superficial—are made in the structure. If substantial changes are not necessary, we make a transcript from the sound recording of the prototype performance and use it as a basis for the creation of a script. Very often, a writer in the group elaborates the script.

EMERGENCE, for instance, has been composed into a full literary piece called KEBUNGKITAN, written in Indonesian verse by Takdir Alisjahbana. When EMERGENCE is produced again, some of these written parts will be used and others will be recreated during each performance through entheotic performing. The score or script for the Ritual performance has to be porous. The same is true for the musical score. Those aspects which require the simultaneous cooperation of many people to carry off a certain effect must be worked out in advance, but it is important to have open space wherever possible for the gods to enter in and speak.

This, to me, is one of the refined challenges of this form of performing—to fix a production so that it can be elaborate and produced many times, but to keep it spontaneous, sufficiently open for the phenomenon of entheotic performing. A formal production is quite a different matter from a "happening" such as we remember from the sixties. The magic of something coming together out of the energy of the moment is utterly essential to vitality and to the visitation of the gods. The opening for the gods has to be maintained.

The form has to be created so that the mystery can continue to arrive. The RITUAL Process then is a delicate dance between creating a structure which allows for an elaborate production, but maintaining the group energy and leaving the form sufficiently open so that the Mothers of Being will come forth to do their healing cathartic work. The tendency is always to overformalize. The craft is to know just how much the tendency to form can be restrained and how much can be left to the gods.

The Spirit of Offering: The Essence of RITUAL

During the expedition to Bali in 1983, when I met with Balinese artists and holy men of the Brahmin caste who were connected with the performing arts, I always posed the question: What is the essence of ritual in Bali? The answer was uniformly the same: offering. The ritual of Bali is always proffered to five essential elements: holy men, ancestors, gods, monsters and all of humanity.

Offering is not just a pious act; it is the spirit with which the ritual is made and performed. It is the basic motivation of the entire enterprise. I am convinced that this was always so, in all sacred traditions. And I believe that it is the spirit of offering that defines ritual. Every effort is made to imbue the RITUAL Stage with this Spirit. When performing art ceases to have offering as its basic motivation, it becomes mere art or entertainment. Offering is indeed the objective essence of ritual.

The objects of the offering are also very significant. From the five essentials in the Balinese offering, I have made the following interpolations. The offering of the RITUAL Stage is made to:

• The Holy Men: those who have reached enlightenment. They represent the possibility of human consciousness. The RITUAL is offered to the highest possible development of consciousness, to the *Enlightened Ones.*

• Ancestors: the archaic predecessors, those who have handed down the pattern of Being. I take it also as the mythos. The RITUAL is offered to the *Archetypes.*

• The Shining Ones or Gods: the great panoply of Balinese gods, the collective Nature Spirits and Magic Helpers, the embassies of the Mothers of Being, the unnamed gods. RITUAL is offered to the *Spirit of Nature.*

• Monsters. The offering represents the attitude appropriate to appeasing the dark force and to transforming the energy of the Monster from its negative form to its harmonious part in the whole. The RITUAL is offered to the *power of the Monster.*

• All of Humanity: the Divine human prototype in all of its individual manifestations—no exceptions. And most of all to its future. The RITUAL is offered to *All of Humanity.*

To these five elements, the entire RITUAL Stage is offered. I have developed various exercises to center the group in this attitude of offering. The primary exercise is practiced at the beginning of each work session following the OM salutation and the RAMs. We sit with our lower arms extended outward, palms facing up in the mudra of offering. I say: "I offer this work to the Enlightened Ones." The group repeats the verbal offering. Then, pressing their hands together above the top of their heads, they make a slow bow to the ground, making a deep internal offering. This obeisance is done four more times: to the Archetypes, to the Spirit of Nature, to the power of the Monster and to All of Humanity. The offering is also part of the group meditation before a performance. Here, what is offered is the performance itself. The offering grounds the entire endeavor, and particularly the performance, in the source from which it comes. When the Initiates are thus grounded, they can become Priests.

The Performers as Priests

When a participant has gone through the Stages of the ORIGINS Process, he has undergone priestly training. Of course, some participants are more gifted that others at this form, but when a participant has remained with the Process, he is usually capable of carrying out the priestly functions in the production of the Ritual.

To really attain priesthood, however, it is important to experience both the Hero's Journey and the Love Story Processes. Each archetype presents a different aspect of transformation, and each represents a distinct approach to the Monster. Going through the Process twice is itself essential. The first time the method itself is such a surprise that one misses many subtleties. The second time, in addition to experiencing the new approach, one has a chance to review the Process and to experience it in a deeper way.

There are about a dozen people with whom I have worked extensively and who have participated in or assisted in many of the trainings. These I would say are the real Priests. The functions and abilities described here are achieved by those who work closely with the Process and experience it from the inside out and the outside in. These Priests are initiated into this path of self-realization and are more or less conversant with the techniques. They can assist on many levels as instructors and counselors for others and can perform as Priest performers.

Comprehension of the Archetypes

The first requirement of a Priest is that he comprehend the archetypes experientially, intellectually and spiritually. Through the successful completion of the DREAM Stage he has a personal comprehension of his own process as expressed through the archetype. Through the DREAM and the MYTH he has an experience of the archetype and its power, and has the opportunity to further transform the ego-Monster. The entire experience is intended to provide him with a personal understanding of the mythos and its expression of the transformation process in all its aspects, from the most personal dream imagery within, to a conceptual understanding of the power of the archetype to express and elicit the transformation. In this way, the Priest comes to know the substance of the unnamed gods.

Mastery of Processing Techniques

Transformation in ORIGINS has been clearly defined in discussing the DREAM Stage. In some ways it is a natural consequence of the application of the archetype. In other ways it is a function of awareness and the use of the techniques provided in the training for transmuting the dross of the ego into the gold of the essence. These techniques must be mastered by the Priest.

Processing the Monster

In the Love Story, the Monster represents a disequilibrium in the balance of receptivity to what is so and appropriate activity. The receptivity is suppressed by fear and lack of trust generated by the Monster. The controlling ego usurps the energy into double-*yang*, thus destroying the balance and maintaining egoistic order by manipulation and control. Processing the Monster means the ongoing use of the authentic methods of transmutation to neutralize the controlling power of the Monster, thereby restoring a balanced responsiveness to the Spirit of Nature and a corresponding capacity for poised action to serve that Spirit.

In the Hero's Journey, the Monster results from the denial by force of some primordial energy or aspect of Being. This energy takes a negative form which pits itself against the conscious being. In this case, the ongoing work of processing the Monster is to release the energy by assimilating the offending aspect as an authentic part of the Self, thereby neutralizing the power of the Monster and accepting it as part of the greater glory of the whole Self.

After the Line exercise is introduced in the MYTH Stage, it becomes the primary means for monitoring the energy of the group. Each conflict that arises between individuals tangibly affects the level of energy. The exercise cleans this interference with the group unity. It also provides insight into the workings of the Monster here/now in this life situation or this performance. Such information is invaluable because it strengthens the Witness by bringing to awareness the activity and power of the Monster as it is actually present and active.

The Monster is also processed by means of the elements of transmutation: awareness, catharsis, love of the Self, and the Magic Implement. The Priest should be completely conversant with the power of these elements and should know how to use them whenever necessary.

The first element is awareness. The Line, the stress of pressure, the confrontation of the performing ego with a situation in which ego-less performance is required, and the production itself (which is dramatizing the transformation process of the group) all serve to heighten awareness of the Monster and the way it works.

Catharsis is the second element. Each Priest should know how to honor and give expression to his feeling without resorting to violence or abuse toward others. He should also be close enough to his authentic emotion that he can bring this authenticity to his performance. But furthermore, the expression of feeling neutralizes the negation that produced the Monster in the first place.

Love for the whole Self is generated through the Process, fostered throughout in the context of the basic attitudinal YES and taught as the basic catalytic agent for transmuting the Monster. There is always some form of up-tightness in the Monster, and Self-love always acts to neutralize that tightness.

When the Myth is created, the group determines one or sometimes several Magic Implements that serve to transform the collective and individual Monsters in the Myth. This, in addition to the Implement received and consecrated in the DREAM, provides a specific catalytic agent for transmuting the energy of the Monster and centering the Priest in the task at hand.

These skills counter the individual Monster in a direct way, serve to process the Monster as it is affecting the group, and often enhance the portrayal of the Monster elements in the Production.

Translation of Awareness into Character and Action

A skill that is unique to the ORIGINS Process is the capacity to translate awareness of Self into characterization and action. This is a very subtle skill requiring great strength of observation and acute perception.

Let us say that a Priestess is playing the Mother of Love. She must be able to look within and see how, in the ongoing tapestry of her own consciousness, the element of loving manifests itself in time of need, in a moment of hopelessness or before the onslaught of an angry impulse. How does it *actually work* in conscious reality? How does it actually neutralize the negative impulses? Then she must see how to bring this awareness into her characterization so that her portrayal becomes more and more accurate to the double it is representing—otherwise the element just proceeds from an idea. The double of the character or the action has to be observed in consciousness, because it is the authentic source of the character or the action.

The Priest-performers are taught a meditation in which they reflect on the aspect they are portraying, reviewing how it has been active during the past day and then seeing how they can bring this new awareness into the characterization. During the preparation of the Ritual, this meditation is practiced once a day.

This skill is critical to the authentication of the piece. It is very difficult, because the Monster strongly influences oversight. That is to say, there is an actual aversion to seeing and observing one's subjective reality with such a magnifying glass. This process progresses like the work of a detective who examines the evidence more and more closely. But it is subtly difficult, because our entire conditioning goes against such close self-inspection.

Part of my work as the High Priest is to monitor this translation, pointing out to a performer that he is not observing sufficiently closely and that his performance does not reflect the truth that he is portraying. Very often I have to go inward myself, find the character element, observe its workings within my own subjectivity and suggest possibilities of characterization to the performer.

When some disorder or dysfunction arises in the group, everyone takes a look at it. Very often there is something there for someone in the group to bring into his portrayal. There are also instances when the performer resorts to a portrayal that has come from his head instead of his awareness. This is usually subtly apparent, and I have to be careful to point out such lapses. All of this is part of monitoring the iconography of the piece.

Mystical Aspects of the Priestly Work

The mastery of processing techniques in the training helps the Priest to deal with the negativity of personal pathology and to clarify the ongoing work of freeing the essence from the ego. But the Priest has to go even further. In order to perform as a pure channel, he has to develop skills that serve him as a human being before the mysteries. The Priest has to become a mystic. In many subtle ways, the entire training points toward this development. In this way, the performer comes to understand the art of performing as a discipline leading to spiritual realization. Wholeness is the condition for the Divine to manifest itself. The experience of wholeness is an experience of God. The authentic holy man is a whole man.

Principles of Aesthetic and Spiritual Balance

Several basic kinds of balance are presented in the trainings: the three centers, activity/receptivity, form and presence. The elements to be balanced differ, but the procedure for balancing them is largely the same. First, each element has to be experienced in its totality. Second, the capacity of each has to be utterly freed and clarified. And third, the element must be brought into harmony with its counterbalancing element.

These states of balance are possible only when the Monster has been transformed, because the energies cannot be balanced if they are blocked or unclear. Balance and the complementary harmony of opposites manifest wholeness and holiness.

Balance of the Three Centers

The balancing of the three centers has been in process from the beginning of the training, starting with the first RAMs. This exercise continues to be the basis of the meditation that opens each work session in the circle.

In the Stages of the training, the repressed body and heart energy is freed as a function of the transmutation of the Monster. As the Monster, this repressed energy has taken a negative and destructive form against the whole. In the transformation, the energy, released from its negativity, returns to its source, the body and the heart.

The release of the mind center happens in a different way. The mind energy does not get repressed, but rather becomes overstressed by the business of maintaining the mental structures which repress and suppress other energies. It guards the feelings of the heart and censors or controls them according to its own prejudgments and fears. It monitors the tension in the body in order to keep it under control. It is a kind of slave driver—Monstrous. When the powerful mental grasp of the Monster is freed up, the mind is also freed from its stressful work.

The energy of each center is also clarified in the Process. Very often someone has a chronic weakness in one of the centers. To work further on the weak center is the responsibility of each Priest. And it is usually clear what kind of work needs to be done. When the body is freed, we become sensitive to its authentic needs. If we can hear, it lets us know when it needs exercise and when it needs rest, what food it really needs, and when it doesn't need to be fed at all. Likewise, when the heart is opened, feeling and intuition are clarified. There is no judgment in the heart, just attraction and non-attraction. It is very pure and wise—beyond the capacity of the mind. The mind reflects and articulates the mythos and the logos. When the mind is clarified, it becomes like the moon reflecting the sun—the primordial knowing of the body and the heart.

The harmonization of these three kinds of energy follows upon their clarification. Where the power of each is free and clear in any given moment, the appropriate energy predominates. It is a natural response to the stimulus of the world. This is what is meant by the balance of the three centers.

In a work of art the aesthetic balance that follows from this harmony gives to each reality its due. The reason that music and movement are so important in the Ritual is because they represent the presence of the heart and body realities. A cerebral, talky play could never be a ritual, precisely because the realities of the other levels are not present.

Balance of Activity and Receptivity

In the Love Story Training, participants are taught about the balance of *yin* and *yang*, active and receptive elements of Being. The two elements have to be freed and clarified before balance can be achieved. This is the purpose of the transformation work in the Love Story and the meditation on the parents that is assigned at the end of the Love Story DREAM.

The *yin*, or receptive capacity, requires complete trust in the universe. It is the basis of the capacity to allow, to be open, to be a channel. This capacity allows the performer to receive the impulse that moves his improvisation; it permits the energy of the body and the heart to express and guide; and it opens the holy man to know the Divine. The holy artist must be able to be totally open and receptive in all three ways. The *yang*, or active capacity, has to be freed as well. This power is freely assertive. It is the capacity for pure action without the adornment of egoistic decoration.

The balance of the active and receptive energies means there is equal capacity to give and to take, to be open and to be closed. There is flexibility. In the life of the priestly performer, both capacities must be there. The active element must be open to the Mothers of Being that allow for presence and authentic spontaneity.

When these capacities are in balance in any given moment, something very magical and truly mystical happens. It is represented by a very slow kind of movement, usually associated with the mastery of Tai Chi. In this motion one experiences being simultaneously moved and moving. It is so subtle that one has to have great awareness of the kinesthesis of movement to experience it at all. It is a pure state of balance between active and receptive energies. There is a poise, a bliss in this state. When the Priest-performers have achieved a sense of this movement and have been well-grounded in the score, they experience this phenomenon on the stage in the Myth and Ritual performance. They are being moved by the power of the archetype and the presence of Divine energy, and their action is totally poised within it. It is a pure state of performing satori.

Balance of Form and Presence

The last principle of aesthetic balance is closely related to this state of blissfully poised movement. It is the balance of form and presence. Again, this balance can be achieved only if the Monster is completely neutralized.

The form comprises either the technique or the score, or both. These have to be mastered so that they can be completely dropped when the Priest enters the Ritual. That is to say, they become second nature, not consciously controlled.

The presence is ability to be totally here/now available to the energy—the god. The body and the form become a vehicle for the animation of the god passing through. The capacity for receiving this energy and becoming its active vehicle is essential to ritual performance. Here again the capacity of the Priest is that of the holy man who, as the Zen writings say, is merely a hollow bamboo through which the Divine passes like music through a flute.

Entheotic Performance

The aspects of the Work of the Priests in the RITUAL Stage are the pre-conditions for entheotic performance:

• The self-absorbed ego must be dealt with authentically so that it no longer has its compulsive need to control and manipulate. This constitutes the substance of the work on the Self through the ORIGINS Process. It is a practical truth in performing and a fundamental spiritual truth that where ego is, the gods cannot be received, nor can they be given utterance.

• The performer and his Work must be offered to the five essentials which together constitute the One. This maintains a right focus for all the Work and performing.

• The performer must have an understanding of and receptivity to the Given, that which is given by the god in the moment of performing. This follows upon the skill of translating awareness into character and action.

• The giving forth of the Given. Being able to translate the Given into pure performing action.

• Achieving balance in the three centers, of the *yin* and *yang*, and between form and presence.

When these conditions are fulfilled, the performer can become a pure channel through which the gods can speak. The performer allows the god in and opens himself completely to the god's expression through him. This is the moment of the *en-theos*, the ecstatic moment when the self of the performer stands out (*ex-stasis*) from the Self and the Self itself becomes the pure vehicle of the god. The archetypal form speaks through that whole and wholly available Self. This is the ecstasy, the fulfillment of the holy performer, the mystical union with the divine through the Ritual.

The difference between improvisation, performing from memory, and entheotic performance may perhaps best be described by a kind of terminology that has developed over the years in dealing with the performers in the process of mastering entheotic performance. We speak of *walking* to describe the experience of performing from rote something that is memorized from before. *Running* describes inspired performing from rote or the kind of let-go experienced in doing the "Ditties" in the CHAOS Stage. *Flying* describes totally inspired memorized performing, or performing the characters in one's Dream, or the psychodrama of the Dream itself when the personal expression of the archetype takes over. At this point one is in the lower order of entheotic performance. The higher order begins to happen in the MYTH Stage and the RITUAL. When one is performing an archetype or god that is transpersonal, especially when there is full orchestration and audience, one can enter *hyperspace*. This is when the grounding of the score is absolutely essential, because one is "gone" in ecstasy. At some level, even the most unpracticed member of the audience is aware of it and resonates to it, because where the performer has "gone" is deep into the inner recesses of the human soul.

My more experienced performers become quite addicted to this place. It is really the "home" of creativity. It is that place of play we knew in childhood innocence. It is the inner place that every performer intuits to be possible, but few have the opportunity to actually experience. It has four components: the creativity of performing as an ordinary craft; the element of receiving and giving as a pure channel; the "primary creativity" usually experienced only by the composer or poet in the moment when the music or text is actually being created for the first time; and union with the Divine.

My sense is that standard performing at its best might provide the experience of the first and a level of the second kind of creativity, but performers are in a sense starved for the third, primary kind of creativity and the union with the Divine that results. This is certainly so for performers who are imbued with both substance and talent, the kind I most enjoy working with. Once they have been in *hyperspace*, why should they want to go back to mere flight? And why should the performers not feel this way? The intuited possibility of such bliss is the reason one is drawn into performing in the first place. This "bliss" is the birthright of the creator. It is that human experience of what the divine creator (and the divine within us) is all about.

I believe that is "Home."

To summarize the preparation of the Priest-performer for his entheotic performance, here are the directions for the meditation as I lead it in preparation for the performance of the Love Story. After costumes, make-up and everything else is in order, the group gathers in a circle. The meditation takes about twenty minutes.

- OM salutation to the One.
- RAMs in the three centers.
- Transformation of Resistance:

–Active: See yourself going through your entire part in the score.

–Receptive: Feel your receptivity to the score, to the group, to the energy of the audience, to the archetype.

–Nature Spirit: See your Nature Spirit. See your Magical Implement. Ask that the power be renewed. Inhale the power into the body, filling the body with the power in three deep breaths.

–Monster: Be aware of any resistance that came up in the active, receptive, or Nature Spirit portions of the meditation. Be aware of any fears or tensions in your body. Be aware of any resistance to giving totally to the performance. See all of these resistances take form as the Monster. Hold up the Magic Implement in front of the Monster. See the Monster losing its form and power, filling you with your total energy and clear capacity to receive and give forth.

- Offering

–Sit in the position of offering.

–Repeat after me: "I offer this performance to the Enlightened Ones." Make a silent internal realization of this offering and then make a bow of obeisance. The group repeats these obeisances to the remaining essentials: the Archetypes, the Spirit of Nature, the power of the Monster, and All of Humanity.

• Om salutation

After this meditation, the Priests remain in objective silence (speaking only when necessary) throughout the performance of the Ritual. Uniformly they become a channel for the archetype, the psyche of the audience, the energy of the present, and the gods who would speak through them.

The Ritual Production

My interest in ritual was kindled long before I had any understanding of its meaning and its value as a model for understanding the original function of theater. In my travels around the world, I have seen many ritual performances. Almost all of them were degenerate forms staged for the benefit of tourists. In Karala I was led on a five-mile trek through the palm jungle to a temple to watch a Katha Kali performance. Non-Hindus were not allowed in the temple, so for a price (about five dollars) they took down a wall so I could watch.

This to me is symbolic of the state of ritual theater in the world. In a sense, any time a non-believer watches a ritual performance, the temple walls are torn down. This is because the basis of the ritual is *the context of belief.* The entire phenomenon has to take place within that context or else the spell is broken. For this reason, I feel that I have never really *experienced* a traditional ritual performance, although I have witnessed many. The revelations I experienced when I first saw the Ramayana performance in Bali were the closest to it, but this was because I broke through the belief context into the actual archetypal level.

Some Principles of Ritual Performance

I have pieced together much about this medium of ritual performance from what I have been able to experience, and I have desired, with a daemonic gravity I can in no way explain, to recreate ritual theater in a context that reaches beyond belief structures or, at least, into the belief structures endemic to this cynical age. To do so I have had to determine features that are common to all ritual theater. Here are some of these principles and some ways that we have used them in our performances.

The Offering of the Ritual Performance

A formal offering is part of ritual performance. Usually, in ritual theater, the high priest performs some sort of ceremony in order to consecrate the space. This consecration sets the scene as the place where the Divine is going to descend to receive the offering.

In Bali, I saw a stunning performance that was staged in a kind of arena space. The musicians sat opposite the audience in the narrower axis of the arena. The shrine of Rangda (the Monster) was to the right of the observers, and the shrine of the Barong (the Nature Spirit) was to the left. There were several priests who consecrated each shrine. They made an animal sacrifice, lit incense and chanted some Sanskrit mantra.

In the RITUAL COMEDY in Amsterdam, the staging was almost identical. The nature kingdom of King Yang and Queen Yin was on one side, and the castle of the Monster Egon was on the other. In the middle was a round mirror on the stage with a single blue spotlight shining down from above and reflecting up out of it. This was the Magic Mirror Lake that had the power to reflect who one really is. After the overture at the beginning, I entered the stage as the High Priest, went to the throne of the Nature Spirit, lit a stick of incense, made an OM salutation, and placed the incense and a flower before the throne. I went to the throne of the Monster and did the same thing. Then I went to the mirror, got down on my knees, polished it until it was spotless, made an OM salutation and left the stage for the performance to begin.

Sometimes an offering is included as the first dance sequence in the ritual. This is standard form in Bali. In our performances in Bali, the dancer or dancers portraying the Nature Spirit opened the performances with a traditional offering dance in which they threw flower petals on the performing area and out into the audience.

The attitude of the offering corresponds in the ORIGINS Process to the basic attitude of YES which stands behind all the work. The YES of existence is the source of creation. The offering of our work of creation is our response in kind. Existence has offered its creation to me: I offer my creation to Existence. There is a deep sense of balance to this.

The Inclusion of Sublime and Comic Elements

One universal element of ritual performance is represented in the Greek tradition by the tragic and comic masks that are associated with the theater today. In *The Birth of Tragedy*, Nietzsche describes the sublime and the comic as ways of transforming the terror and the absurdity of existence.

The sublime "subjugates terror by means of art." I am reminded of the healing work of the shaman who transforms the non-assimilable experiences of psychic terror into a form or cosmos by which that experience becomes assimilated. Likewise, art gives sublime or symbolic form to the psyche rendered chaotic by the "terror" of Dionysian chaos. The art form provides to a psyche traumatized by the fear of existence a symbolic language by which the incomprehensible can be comprehended and inexpressible states can be expressed. This expression induces the release of the healing process by ordering it into intelligible form.

The *comic* element "releases us through art from the tedium of absurdity." Here we must consider the power of humor as a transforming element. Whenever I can laugh at my situation, recognize myself in the comical situation of another, many things happen. For one, the Witness is strengthened. A new distance is created from my situation. Humor often results from the arrival of a new perspective and is in fact a way of dealing with the inconsistency of two kinds or levels of perspective. Integrating new perspectives frees us from the identification which might otherwise create suffering. Furthermore, laughter activates body energies which get depressed in identification. There are many new scientific studies that demonstrate the power of humor to reverse actual pathologies in the body. I sometimes have my groups laugh for five minutes. By the end of that time, everyone is splitting their sides over the mutual infectiousness of each other's laughter. It changes the entire energy of the group.

Humor is always an important aspect of ritual drama. In the long Balinese temple dramas, there are standard comic figures who carry on for hours before the heavy confrontations begin to come down. This humor functions to prepare the psyche for transformation.

The sublime and comic spirits serve man in the supreme "jeopardy of the will" that constitutes human existence. "Art, that sorceress expert in healing, approaches him; only she can turn his fits of nausea into imaginations with which it is possible to live" (Nietzsche, *The Birth of Tragedy*). These imaginations are generated by the interplay of the sublime and comic spirits. Both are necessary and a balance between them is essential.

The Context of Living Myth

In order for the participating audience to resonate into the ritual drama, they must feel invested in the performance with a deep existential sense of involvement and connectedness. Insofar as the ritual is subjectively determined by this audience, it requires a specifically local viability informed by universal truths.

In traditional ritual theater, the symbols are already implanted in the psyche of the community by virtue of the fact that the community has been brought up in them. In Bali, for instance, Rangda the Monster is part of the fabric of the society's self identification. Rangda is a living mythical symbol. When she clatters through the streets of the village, everyone is genuinely terrified.

The fact that elsewhere these traditional symbols are no longer alive, no longer charged with overwhelming identification, accounts in large part for the demise of ritual performance. My hypothesis is, however, that a relevant archetypal symbol readily recognized by any human being can serve in the same way. In EMERGENCE, when the red figure of the Greed for Power was leaping wildly around the stage with a bomb-shaped toy in his hand marked H, everyone in the audience knew who he was, and their response was similar to that evoked by Rangda. I believe it is possible to generate symbols that are universally quickening.

The fact of the matter is that the unconscious hungers for authentic expression of the archetypes. This is why we keep going to see the same basic story over and over again. We hunger for a conscious vision of our necessary unconscious processes. This chronic need for Myth is only partially met in our time. It is, as Jung said, a substantial factor in the pathology of the modern soul. The fact that we have no unifying mythology does not mean that the internal movement of the mythos that expresses itself in myth is not operating. It simply means that it is not finding any unitary expression or deriving the satisfaction it requires.

What has to be expressed in the Myth and portrayed in the Ritual is the present existential and psychic reality of the audience. The human characters have to be involved in dilemmas that are pertinent to the present circumstances of those in the audience, and the superhuman characters have to accurately express the greater powers by which they are being moved. The audience should be involved sympathetically, empathetically, existentially, psychologically and psychically. The more of these levels that are engaged, the more powerful the cathexis, the connection of symbol and reality. But true cathexis has to happen by virtue of the same marriage of symbol and content that happens when we dream, though instead of the psyche evoking the symbol, the symbol must evoke the psyche.

Finally, the Myth in the ritual should somehow include a vision of optimal human development. The hero who dies before he achieves the boon may make for true drama of our time, but it won't do for ritual. The ritual must show the entire cycle of separation, initiation and return. The lovers who never get it together may be poignantly true to life, but in the Myth they must be united, even if, as in Tristan and Isolde, their union happens in death. The completion of the cycle is essential. Unlike degenerated entertainment forms, the performance is not merely depicting a realistic situation; through the ritual, it is recreating the alchemy of transformation.

The Authentic Transmutation of the Monster

The Monster in the ritual has to be the real Monster of the audience, and the ritual has to portray with authenticity the transmutation of the Monster and the victory of the Spirit of Nature. This is always done with great craft in the original rituals that I have seen. It is the greatest challenge in the RITUAL. If it is hokey, the ritual falls flat. How does the Hero authentically use the Magic Implement to overcome the Monster and wrest from him the power which is his?

In Bali this is accomplished in an amazing and powerful way in the Barong ritual. In the battle of the Barong and Rangda, the Barong calls forth his helpers, devotees in costume who enter a real trance and move toward Rangda with drawn knives. Rangda casts an evil spell over them that causes them to turn the knives inward toward their own breasts. This spectacle of self-destruction is wild. Since the helpers are in a trance, they are quite unconscious of what is happening. The priests make more offerings, and the Barong then casts another spell over the helpers that shields them and prevents the knives from tearing into their breasts. This is taken as a victory.

Rangda often escapes and disappears into the fields around the village. The audience understands that even though her return is inevitable, her evil energy has once more been usurped and turned to protect the soul of man. This catharsis is genuine and affects the entire village.

The Enchantment of the Audience

The authenticity of the Monster and the relevance of the myth engage the audience. The ways and means of enchanting the audience are probably the most critical aspect of ritual theater. This enchantment is what I experienced years ago in Bali at the performance of the Ramayana. At that time I realized that this feature of ritual was its essential power.

The enchantment in the ritual is the antithesis of "proscenium" and "mask." In traditional entertainment, these constitute a barrier. An illusion is created that is set before an audience which is entirely passive to it. The story may of course engage the audience, but it is somehow happening "out there." The illusion serves this "out there" quality of the production. Empathy, sympathy, recognition are all valid forms of involvement, but in ritual there is another order of engagement. There may in fact be a proscenium (that is to say, a place where the audience ends and the stage area begins) and the performers may indeed wear masks. But there can never be a psychological barrier. In ritual, this psychological distance has to disappear.

In ritual theater, the characters and the action are the double of the mythic archetypal constituents of the psyche. The characters symbolically represent actual aspects of the collective (and individual) psyche of the audience. The ritual works only when there is an actual nexus of symbol and double in which they become one. Likewise the interaction of the characters and the action of the piece must become one with the actual archetypal movement within the psyche. This is why I say rhetorically that proscenium and mask have to disappear. One could say equally that they must act to propel the symbolic characters and the action into that place where the symbol and its double become one. However it is expressed, that is the crux of ritual.

There are a number of factors other than the authenticity of the myth and its Monster that influence the happening by which outer theater and inner drama become one. The first is the alteration of the consciousness of the audience. This is accomplished in a number of ways. Here are some techniques I have observed and others we have tried:

One of the most powerful methods for altering consciousness is fatigue. The coherent waking consciousness is in league with the proscenium and has to be broken down. Fatigue works like a charm. This is probably one reason Richard Wagner, himself a ritual maker, made his productions five to ten hours in length. The temple performances in Bali and in India hardly ever begin before eleven in the evening. Very often, they begin even later. If they do begin before midnight, there may be hours of elaborate story infused with all sorts of comic acts before the heavy stuff begins, that is, before the actual apotheosis of the Monster and the Spirits of Nature.

A second factor is music. The gamalan of Bali and Java is absolutely spellbinding. Whenever I hear it, I get chills all up and down my spine and often find myself sobbing for no apparent reason. My sense is that it strikes the sensitive centers (chakra points) on the spine and quickens the corresponding levels of consciousness. I believe this factor as much as any other caused my experience with the Ramayana in Bali.

We have experimented with many musical forms and types of music. Some have been very powerful and effective, especially those that use conga drums. I have found that the essential element in the music is percussion and rhythm. It is said in many primitive tribes that the gods are in the drums. My drummer friends corroborate this. Functionally speaking, the drums can alter consciousness. We had a whole orchestra of congas for a production that was done in Big Sur, and it cast a wildly hypnotic spell. But the most powerful music of all was the twenty-five piece gamalan orchestra in Bali. Performing on stage with them was like being in a high voltage electrical current. Being in the audience was almost the same. It definitely alters consciousness.

Less powerful, but equally important, is setting. The setting needs to create a continuum from the source, out to and encompassing the audience. The audience needs to be brought into the embrace of the action, not excluded and set outside. Theaters usually have the effect of abstracting the audience from the scene. There is, on the other hand, something undeniably engaging about a temple in the middle of the night surrounded by primordial trees, with the torches throwing strange shadows over the scene.

It can transport you to another dimension. I have never experienced this kind of transport in a theater. The setting of the ritual needs to encompass the audience as well as the performance.

The Myth that was performed in the garden in Hollywood was inspired by the most exciting setting I have ever experienced. It was in Ramnagar across the Ganges from Banaras. I was once invited there by the Maharajah to participate in the production of the *Ram Lila*. This production, performed yearly, lasts for six weeks! About three scenes from the Ramayana are played each day. Every one of them is performed in a different sacred place, either in the palace of the Maharajah or in the enormous forest and wilderness that surround the place. The party is transported to each scene riding on elephants in a procession. The procession includes the performers, the bearers of their costumes and props. The Maharajah on his elephant is followed by the elephants of the guests and finally by the populace carrying torches. It is an incredible spectacle. The pace is very slow, but the cumulative effect is amazing.

Another effective method is the use of drugs. Bhang, a drink made from cannabis, is used in India on certain festivals. In a few Myth productions when the audience was small, we have tried passing a peace pipe and found that it works very effectively.

A final method is audience participation. We have tried countless experiments involving the participation of all or some members of the audience. Some devices have been more effective than others. In general, though, I would say that unless the audience knows what it is doing and why, such activities tend to distract them. Their involvement, the cathexis with the double, is actually hindered rather than enhanced.

Another factor that affects the phenomenon of cathexis is to engage the audience through all three centers. Just as the gongs in the gamalan affect certain centers along the spine, so certain instruments affect the body center (drum, percussion, base, tuba), the heart center (violin, flute, harp) and the mind center (song, spoken words). In many productions these have been orchestrated in certain ways so as to involve the audience at all of these levels.

The three centers can also be engaged by the quality of the action. Music itself engages the heart and the body; dance engages the body; song engages the heart. This is why the multi-media approach is particularly suited for contemporary ritual theater. Different media affect different centers.

All of these methods and elements create enchantment. Speaking of Greek theater, Nietzsche, in the *Birth of Tragedy,* elaborates on the idea of the satyr:

> Enchantment is the precondition of all dramatic art. In this enchantment, the Dionysian reveler sees himself as satyr, and as satyr, in turn he sees the god. In his transformation he sees a new vision, which is the Apollonian completion of his state. And by the same token this new vision completes the dramatic act.

Enchantment is the ground possibility for ritual performance to complete its function. Through enchantment, the participant, the "Dionysian reveler" (the player first, and by extension the enchanted audience), enter the state of the satyr. That is, he becomes the expression of the Mothers of Being. Becoming one with the Mothers, he glimpses the ineffable Divine. Or, merging with the dynamic of nature, he has an experience of oneness; he "sees the god."

This state constitutes a transformation in which a new vision is seen. This new vision of wholeness through the dream, the myth, is the "Apollonian completion" of the process of transformation. The new state is given a form by which it becomes viable and lasting. This, Nietzsche says, "completes the dramatic act." That is to say, it fulfills the function of the ritual drama—psychologically, spiritually and aesthetically.

The RITUAL Performance

The productions that we have created in the RITUAL have varied according to the requirements of the group and the production. The Process works very effectively as a method for generating a certain spirit and a content that reflects the Self of the group and the community it represents. If we have a group with a definite purpose and a small budget, our production conforms to those parameters. If we have a large budget and an open-ended group, our production will reflect those circumstances. Everything varies according to the requirements, the nature of the artists participating, the talent of the group and the available resources.

From the point of view of production, a definite advantage of the ORIGINS method is speed. Although it goes back to the Source, a production can be conceived, created and produced in a remarkably short time. In Bali the performers told us that we accomplished in about twenty days what would normally take six months. The slower pace of Asia notwithstanding, I believe it is safe to say that the entire process of creating a production is about half of what it would be for a scripted production created by a standard process.

In part, the effectiveness and speed with which the piece comes together is because the Process works with clean, as opposed to neurotic, energy. All the ego trips that normally plague a production are made part of the Process and fed, in a healthy way, into creating the piece. Instead of being a drain on the energy as it usually is, the power of the ego-Monsters has a much greater chance of being recycled into an energy that furthers the production.

There is also a sense of self-fulfillment experienced by everyone in the group. At the end they feel that tremendous growth has taken place. As a performer, it is incredibly fulfilling to play one's inner self. There is a connectedness between who one really is and what one is portraying that yields a level of artistic and spiritual fulfillment for the performer that many say they have never experienced before.

The ORIGINS Process generates a content of image and act, Myth and Ritual. This content can be brought into any kind of production. It may be anything from a standard proscenium theater piece or a full-length feature film to all sorts of experimental productions involving the application of the principles of ritual theater and entheotic performance.

In the "ordinary production" category, we have done several video-dramas in Los Angeles and Canada and two standard theatrical productions performed by clowns in Vancouver. I would say that these productions manifest a certain awareness of the archetypal content which differs from other kinds of theatrical and film productions. It is as though the story were turned inside out. The inner meaning of the characters and action is emphasized as opposed to the mere story or the issues with which the story is imbued by virtue of its circumstances and its setting. Also because of the method of creating the piece there is a unique freshness to the performing. There is a blood, a spirit that is not present in productions that are created in a standard way.

One of the most interesting and unusual standard type of productions has been based on the actual Dream Stage of the Love Story. This play is not the result of the entire ORIGINS Process, but is rather adapted from the actual process of Tom, whose performance transcript was analyzed in the discussion of the DREAM Stage. Entitled TRANSEX: *The Transformation of a Transvestite*, it is a scripted, two-character play which does not include entheotic performance.

I am always interested in ways of generating productions from this Process, but I believe that the Process is actually fulfilled by Ritual Performance—that which has flowered since the expedition to Bali in 1983 and adheres to the principles of ritual performance. Mere theater is simply too thin a medium to suffice as ritual. Such ritual performance must always include both music and entheotic performing.

Music simply transports. In Nietzsche's words, "it incites the audience to a symbolic intuition of a Dionysian universality." It has the capacity to stun us with mythical affect. It also endows symbolic image with supreme significance. As I experiment more and more with music, I find that certain forms of music affect the Dionysian by overwhelming the individual consciousness. In Nietzsche's terms, it expresses "the omnipotent will of Being behind individuation."

There are two long-term projects that I have been cultivating over the last few years, both of which have a very prominent musical base.

The first of these is the Bali project. In 1987 I returned with another group of American performers to the Toya Bungkah Center to co-create with Takdir Alisjahbana a second dance drama. This one is based on the Love Story. Its theme is the coming together of the East and the West into one world. It is called CONVERGENCE. This production, together with EMERGENCE, forms a package. In these two pieces the gamalan orchestra creates the powerful and transformational musical base that I have already discussed in describing the creation of EMERGENCE.

The second project is a new departure into productions with a radical musical base, two full-on operas: THE LIGHT OPERA from the Hero's Journey and THE GRAND OPERA from the Love Story. Both of these operas are fundamental myths—that is, basic human stories which are universal and which can be understood by any human being the world over. We call them "THE ORIGIN OPERAS." Here, the entheotic performance of music reaches its ultimate manifestation.

THE LIGHT OPERA

By way of concluding the description of the RITUAL Stage, here is a description of THE LIGHT OPERA.

THE LIGHT OPERA dramatizes the epic of the human spirit in its relationship to the eternal Mother Light. Tibetan sound implements, piano, organ and other classical instruments together with four female voices express the Light of human consciousness.

Light has been played by a singer of eighty years. Her magnificent and mature voice is contrasted with that of three other women. The second character, Truth, is portrayed by one of the most practiced ORIGINS performers who is a virtual adept at entheotic performance. She is a musical genius and can produce an aria at the drop of a hat. She is the voice coach for the opera. It is primarily because of her that I had courage to attempt an opera in the first place, and she has supported and exemplified the possibility of such an opera from the very beginning. Her name is Sarah Light. The third character, portrayed by a very powerful and talented singer, new to ORIGINS but ancient in her understanding, portrays the Dark One, the Monster who causes us to forget our Light source. The fourth character, the Spirit, is portrayed by the daughter of Sarah Light, a brilliant and versatile young performer who is also one of the most experienced ORIGINS performers. The four women are almost equally distributed in and between eighty and twenty-five. The four voices differ significantly because of the age differences. These differences in voice quality have a definite dramatic significance in the work.

The opera lasts about an hour. It evokes the essential drama, the journey of the Heroic human spirit: the source of the Spirit in the Eternal Light of consciousness; the irresistible separation and fall into the egoistic world of the Dark One; the realization of death; and the powerful return to the Light. It is a kind of pre-Christian Mystery play and has been staged most powerfully in a Gothic cathedral.

Here is the score showing how the characters, basic story, basic blocking and musical themes and notations are set. The rest is entheos—the music, now wild and surging like Wagner, now lyrical like Mozart, now haunting like Debussy, now chaotically atonal like Schoenberg, now blues, now rock 'n' roll. Each of these musical styles has its own expressive and dramatic value. The experience is luminous, intense and deeply, powerfully expressive.

LIGHT OPERA Score

Music Notes: The music should be gorgeous and sumptuous. Each section should begin with the instrument that is to predominate in that section. Other instruments come in as appropriate.

Scene	Words	Actions	Music
Intoning	"In the beginning, Being and Light are one."		
Overture			Tibetan sound implements and organ swell
MYSTERIUM			
Light	Light aria	Light introduces Truth	Rhapsodic scale progression
Truth	"I am the daughter of light. What is this story?"		Wagnerian
The Dark One	Darkness aria		Percussion, gong, 60-sec intro, Berg
MYSTERIUM (beginning of action)			
Light and Being			Light major
	Being aria		up-tempo
			Mozart
	B: "I want to be a light of my own."		
	B and L duet		
	L: "Yes, you may go. You will retain my essence, but you will forget."		
Truth enters	L introduces Truth		
	L: "Truth will help you remember me. You will take a form of many colors."		
		L places shawl on B	
	T explains shawl and capacity to choose her or not.		
	L & T, Remember duet		Remember theme
		L sits on throne	
EARTH			
	Being arietta, "Happy to be here."		
		Seduction of Being	Seductive, Spanish

	D gives boa	
Money	Gambling	Piano music
	in a casino	
Power	D introducing Miss Glory	Blues
	B: "I'm the best."	
	D brings men	Happy and frivolous
Light intervenes		
	L and T duet	
	L: "My child is separate from me. As often as I have seen this, there is pain in the universe."	
	T: "Love can bring her back."	"Love can bring her back" theme
	L & T: "Love is the return to light."	
	T brings Lover	
Love	T Remember theme (L in background)	Debussy waltz
	B waltz aria	Remember theme
	B: "Something I remember."	
Betrayal	D arranges that Lover rejects B for another woman	Berg
	B: confusion	Scriabin
	D: gloating over betrayal	
	D: Nothing aria	
		Wild, polytonal
	D envelops her in cloak	
	B: torment	
Remembrance	L sends Truth to Being	Remember theme
	Now she can see who she is.	
	Through nothing, Being can see the light.	
	T: Remember aria	
Battle	D and T	Sound implements

			vs piano
Awakening	Silence	B awakens	
	B: "I see who you are."	D turns, wearing	
		Death Mask	
Return	B, L, T trio		Ecstatic
	D: "So, you think I am defeated.		
	I've got you all!"		
	L, B, T Remember		
	Moment of silence		
Intoning	"In the beginning, light and being		
	are one."		Gong

THE LIGHT OPERA is just the beginning of the exploration of the possibilities of entheotic music. The productions of THE LIGHT OPERA have proven to me that the vehicle can fly. I know that if it can fly, it can hit hyperspace. The music is already something unique, but I envision vast possibilities.

Entheotic music comes out of the deep archaic past of humanity, but it can now be augmented infinitely because of two factors. We have unprecedented sophistication because we have access to music from all over the world and all of musical history in which music was scored and can be reproduced. Added to this is all the possibilities resulting from sound and musical technology. When the requisite talents are there with sufficient training and preparation, the world will hear stunning music of a power and otherworldly magnificence unequalled by anything from the past.

The real power is the *theos* in entheotic performance, through which it is possible to create the critical place in music where art and spirit touch and become one. For the entheotic performer, his art is the form and his emptiness is the possibility of the fullness of spirit. For the performance, art itself is the form and spirit is the force.

In the Ritual Productions the Dionysian energy and the Apollonian form come together in dramatic action. The following quotation from *The Birth of Tragedy* is Nietzsche's description of this possibility of ritual performing art and its capacity to hurl us into the Origins:

Dionysian art...wishes to convince us of the eternal delight of existence, but it insists that we look for this delight not in the phenomena but behind them. It makes us realize that everything that is generated must be prepared to face its painful dissolution. It forces us to gaze into the horror of individual existence yet without being turned to stone by the vision: a metaphysical solace momentarily lifts us above the whirl of shifting phenomena. For a brief moment we become, ourselves, the primal Being, and we experience its insatiable hunger for existence. Now we see the struggle, the pain, the destruction of appearances, as necessary because of the constant proliferation of forms pushing into life, because of the extravagant fecundity of the world will. We feel the furious prodding of this travail in the very moment in which we become one with the immense lust for life and are made aware of the eternity and indestructibility of that lust. Pity and terror notwithstanding, we realize our great good fortune in having life—not as individuals, but as part of the life force with whose procreative lust we have become one.

Summary: RITUAL

Epilogue

A true sacred performing art of the future most certainly has to do with a return to the blood of humanity. As the blood is to the body, so the essence of Being is to the human being. A sacred performing art expresses the essence of the human prototype, and thus of all human beings.

This has been my vision for ORIGINS.

The source of blood cells is the marrow of the pelvic bone and femur. The blood originates in the body center, the source of life—the place of the Mothers.

Just so, sacred performance should originate out of the source of life itself. It should come from the Earth, from the body which is the knowing seat of the unconscious. It should be an oracular, prophetic form.

As the blood eliminates waste and protects the body, so the essence of Being eliminates the dysfunctions of human reality, protects the human prototype and each one of us.

Accordingly, sacred performance should inquire into the real nature of the Monster and provide a cathartic process by which evil can be eliminated. The art form must serve awareness of what is evil; it must show how the Monster is to be understood in a time of profound cultural shift when all things are ambiguous, and it must present the means by which the Monster can be authentically transmuted. For this we have to understand the Monster at an individual level, at a collective level and at the level of the one planet.

In the RITUAL COMEDY in Amsterdam, the Monster was portrayed as Egon, a sort of malignant deformation in human consciousness of the *yang* principle that would gain complete control and obliterate the *yin* principle. His sisters were Cynica and Maya, two Monsters in drag.

In the Ritual ballet EMERGENCE created in Bali, the Monster was the Greed for Power. With his great Bomb, his project was to destroy the planet. The religious bigot, the dictator, the business exploiter and the mad scientist were all his minions. They all wore his masks. The Supreme Ordeal of the artist hero was precipitated by his recognition that the Monster of the world is also deep within himself. This is where the Monster must be dealt with. The first theater is the inner one.

As the blood carries food to the cells of the body, so the essence of Being nourishes and regenerates humanity. Likewise, sacred performance should express a universal essence. For this reason the ORIGINS Process was based upon the archetypes and is intended to *divine* that which is universal in all human beings. Sacred performance should be a way of communing with this universal expression. The international experiments in Indonesia and Amsterdam have given a glimpse of how such a form can unify individuals and national groups and, most assuredly, nations themselves, by expressing authentic factors which bind all human beings as one.

Like the blood, the human prototype is more fundamental than any human difference. The Divine human prototype expresses not the average, debased, lowest common denominator of humanity, but its deepest essence and its highest possibility. This was represented in EMERGENCE by the artist Hero who, penetrating deep into his own chaos, could come to terms with the existential fear of Nothingness behind the Greed for Power and transmute the might of that demon in such a way as to fill out his own totality as a human being. The bodhisattva artist has found his own wholeness and is thus a visionary for a whole planet.

This regeneration mirrors the true function of the blood. The transformation is the way of the performer as the pathfinder for the audience. The performer and his transformation are the prototype for the transformation of the community. Through the Ritual that he creates out of his own Dream and Myth, the Priest shows the way, the dharma.

In EMERGENCE the artist uses the power of the Spirits of Nature to overcome the Monster within, and with the help of the Mother of Love, to transform Greed into care. In the RITUAL COMEDY it was the heroic task of the human Hero to restore the balance of *yin* and *yang* in the universe by seeing in the Magic Mirror Lake the vision of his own feminine nature, which then empowered King Yang to rescue his Queen Yin from the cruel oblivion of Egon.

These stories of transformation are prototypes of a world mythology. They express values, goals and aspirations of a planetary culture which are equally viable for an individual. What is valuable and true for any human being in a world view is so for any other human being. In the RITUAL COMEDY the power was placed in the Magic Mirror Lake, that image of the pure Witness, the eye of God, into which any man can look and see with clarity who he authentically is and what the true issues are. In EMERGENCE the power came from the Mother of Love. To strengthen the Hero for his task she sent the Spirit of Air and Water who gave him the magic shell bearing the truth that all men are the expression of God. She sent the Spirit of Fire and Earth with a flower to empower him with the insight that we come from nature and are responsible for nature. These Magic Implements express essential human values, the authentic transforming elements that come through love and awareness. They work. They are the real hope for a planet in peace.

Finally and ultimately, the blood brings the vital essence from the air and transforms it into the vitality of the body. This essence, called oxygen by our scientists and *prana* by the mystics of India, is brought through the lungs into the blood, pumped into the heart and sent out into the entire body. Just so the essence of Being is breathed moment to moment into the human being.

The essence, the truth of Being, is the nameless God. It has not yet been named, and the old names defile its true Mystery.

In the Myths and Rituals of Bodhisattva Arts and ORIGINS we have named many names: King Yang and Queen Yin, the Mother of Love, the spirits Urge and Sol are but a few. In the time of the double not, when the gods reign beyond the vision of our eyes and the capacity of our images and words, the names do not and cannot matter. What is to be evoked in the Myth and worshipped in the Ritual are the true forms which remain hidden in Mystery. A specific religion does not matter, nor does a specific Myth or Ritual. They are but fingers pointing to the moon. What matters is to *let* them indicate the moon—to let the form give authentic expression to the faceless One that remains in Mystery.

The art of the future and the religion of the future will give birth to each other out of the common Origins. From this birth will come forth the name of the God of a new world order. We are all the divine human prototype. The bodhisattva is our hope, our vision, our savior. It is the divine human prototype realizing itself in its wholeness and revealing itself so that we may all be One.

Chronology of Bodhisattva Arts and ORIGINS Productions

December 1978	Los Angeles	*The Ramayana: A Dance Ritual* Continuum Studio
August 1979	Los Angeles	*The Story of Ram: An Alchemical Drama* Grace Cathedral
July 1980	San Diego	*The Androgyny Ritual* International Androgyny Conference
March 1981	Los Angeles	The March Project: *A Nature Ritual* Nichols Canyon Gardens
		Angeline Devine: A Hollywood Fable Videodrama
		The Divine Androgyne: A Rock Ritual Ocean Park Church
May 1981	Topanga, CA	*The Story of Betty and Sammy:* *A Chaotic Comedy* Bodhisattva Theater
July 1981	Maui, Hawaii	*Mega* One Earth Gathering Seabury Hall
January 1982	Los Angeles	The Psyche Plays: *Psyche Drama* *Psyche Duet* Burton Chase Park Theater Videodrama: Valley Cable
April 1982	Vancouver, Canada	*Circus! A Clown Play in Three Acts* Firestation Theater

June 1982	Vancouver, Canada	*Ebb and Flo: An ObsceneDrama* Firestation Theater Videodrama
August 1982	Topanga, California	*Yoni and Phallus: A Tantric Comedy* Bodhisattva Theater
September 1982	Los Angeles	*John Hero: A Video Adventure* Rajneesh Shakespeare Group Communicon Cable Company
October 1982	Los Angeles	*Two Love Stories* One Act Plays Burton Chase Park Theater
November 1982	Los Angeles, Laguna, San Diego, California	*A Divine Comedy* Rajneesh Meditation Centers
December 1982	Malibu, California	*A Woman's Saga* A Living Story in a Woman's Home
February 1983	Bali, Indonesia	*Emergence: A Dance Drama* (I) Balai Seni Toyabungkah, Ubud
October 1983	Amsterdam, Holland	*Lovers: A Ritual Comedy* The Kosmos
June 1985	Hollywood, California	*Light Opera* (I) The First Improvisational Opera
May 1986	Santa Monica, California	*The Light Opera* (II) St. Augustine's By The Sea
March 1987	Bali, Indonesia	*Convergence: A Dance Ritual* Art Center, Den Pasor
March 1988	Bali, Indonesia	*Emergence: A Dance Drama* (II) Art Center, Den Pasor
March 1989	Bali, Indonesia	*Convergence: A Dance Ritual* (II) Balai Sini Toyabungkah

November 1989	Vienna, Austria	*Die Liebenden: Eine Reise in den Traumton*
April 1990	Bali, Indonesia	*Emergence (III)* Balai Sini Toyabungkah
August 1990	Findhorn, Scotland	*PAN!* Botanical Gardens, Edinburgh Festival
August 1990	Edinburgh, Scotland	*The Light Opera* The Great Cathedral of Edinburgh

Glossary

Androgyne (lit. man-woman): The human being who has realized and balanced, within, the full possibilities of active and receptive modes of being.

Androgynous: Having equally balanced masculine and feminine characteristics.

Apollo: Greek god of reason, dream and the principle of individuation. His Oracle was at Delphi.

Apollonian: Organizing principle of the Self and of dream, the light, the rational.

Arica: A mystical school whose Teaching-Master, Oscar Ichazo, synthesized many meditation, awareness and physical exercises into one comprehensive system. Based in New York City.

Bodhisattva: One who has the possibility to achieve or who has achieved full awareness, wholeness, or enlightenment and who chooses to remain working among the suffering of the world.

Bodhisattva Arts: Earlier (1980–1985) name of ORIGINS.

Catharsis: The full expression of suppressed or repressed feelings or emotion. An essential element in Greek drama.

Cathexis: The fixing of desire or meaning on some object or person.

Dionysus: Ancient Greek god of the irrational, the passionate, the instinctual, the drunken.

Dionysian: Instinctual, animal, natural, drunken, wild, passionate.

Ego: Used in the Eastern sense meaning that which sees itself as separate from the ground of Being.

Enlightenment: The ultimate knowing, the flowering of consciousness into its highest awareness.

Entheotic performing: Performing in a high state of being, or trance. The controlling ego of the performer is put aside and the "god" or archetype expresses itself through the performer. A form of high improvisation.

Expressive arts therapies: Therapies which employ artistic creativity as a medium for Self-awareness and healing.

Gestalt: A therapeutic term referring to the configuration of the whole in any given moment.

213

Gestalt therapy: A therapeutic procedure in which the patient is facilitated to complete some as yet unrealized or unexpressed part of himself.

Hero: The character in the Love Story Process that represents the *yang* or Active Principle of the Self.

Heroic Person: The character in the Hero's Journey Process who represents the *yang*, adventurous, goal-oriented aspect of the personality. May be represented as either male or female.

Heroine: The character in the Love Story Process that represents the *yin* or Receptive Principle of the Self.

Host: The individual whose Self is constellated by the characters in the Process. The "I" who is undergoing the Process.

Hubris: The pride of the ego in asserting itself over the Whole, thereby subjecting itself to the wrath of the rejected. A theme central to Greek Tragedy and in the ORIGINS Process.

Imago Dei: The image of God. The image or symbol of the wholeness of the individual consciousness and the consciousness of all. The image that arises out of the psyche or the civilization that expresses the fulfillment of individuation.

Individuation: The fundamental process and pattern of psychic growth by which the self flowers into its own unique realization of the Self or wholeness.

Initiate: A participant in the ORIGINS Process who has been initiated into the secrets of the archetype through his participation in the CHAOS and DREAM Stages.

Maenads: Ancient Greek word for female devotees of Dionysus. Earthly representatives of the Mothers of Being.

Monster: The archetypal figure in the ORIGINS Process which represents the negative ego of the participant and later of the group.

Mothers of Being: The forceful regulators of the Center of Nature.

Mystery: The mysterious realms of Being out of which emerge our Being and the symbols by which we can interpret its meaning.

Myth: The expression of the truth of Being in story.

Mythos: The realm of the collective and individual psyche out of which emerges the symbols and stories by which the psyche can know itself.

Nature Spirit: The archetypal character who represents the benign power of nature and of individuation.

Neophyte: A participant in the DREAM Stage of the ORIGINS Process. One who is "newly planted" in the secrets of inner surrender.

Objective: That which pertains to the collective human consciousness or the divine human prototype.

Paradigm: A basic model or pattern of preconceptions, a substream of ideas.

Phallus: The symbol of the erect penis, sometimes called a *lingum*.

Priest: A participant in the RITUAL Stage of the ORIGINS Training. One who has sufficient experience of the archetype to take responsibility for setting it forth.

Process: (1) The way in which individuation happens uniquely to an individual; (2) the stages of the ORIGINS Training.

Resistance: The inability to surrender to one's essence; inhibition.

Ritual: The fourth Stage of the ORIGINS Process, in which the group Myth is prepared into a production for public presentation.

Sacred: That which expresses or pertains to the mystical essence of human consciousness.

Sadhana: Sanskrit word for personal spiritual discipline or path.

Samadhi: Sanskrit word for a deep state of meditative tranquility.

Satori: Japanese word for a deep state of meditative tranquility.

Satyr: Half-man, half-goat figure in Greek mythology who worships Dionysus. Represents the instinctual level of human beings.

Self: With small "s," the ego self, ego identity or individual personality which longs for but often conceals the Self. With capital "S,"the total human possibility which is the same for all, but uniquely manifest in each.

Subjective: The reality of the ego or self.

Structuralism: An approach taken across many disciplines which looks to correspondences between systems to understand the behavior of their parts. Dating from the 1950s, the approach has been most widely explored by French intellectuals.

Tantra: The most ancient, and still prevalent, path to enlightenment through surrender. It views the ultimate achievement as wholeness rather than as achieving an ideal. This approach is becoming more prevalent in Western psychology and spiritual disciplines, particularly in California. Its traditional forms are still widely practiced in certain sects of Hinduism and Buddhism.

Transpersonal therapy: A therapeutic approach which proceeds from the assumption that psychological well-being has to do with the relationship to the divine, which is beyond the personal. The psychology of the divine human prototype and its therapeutic practices.

Transformation: (1) Any significant psychological change; (2) the change from an idealistic mode of being to a wholeness mode.

Yang: The active or male principle, complementary to *yin*.

Yin: The receptive or female principle, complementary to *yang*.

Yoga: The way of the will, in contrast to the way of Tantra, or surrender. Achieving an ideal state (union with the Divine) through discipline of the self, and the practices that are conducive to that union.

Zeitgeist: The spirit of the times.